AN ILLUSTRATED GUIDE TO
MODERN NAVAL
AVIATION
AND AIRCRAFT CARRIERS

AN ILLUSTRATED GUIDE TO

MODERN NAVAL
AVIATION
AND AIRCRAFT CARRIERS

John Jordan

PRENTICE HALL PRESS
New York   London   Toronto
Sydney   Tokyo

A Salamander Book

Prentice Hall Press
Gulf + Western Building
1 Gulf + Western Plaza
New York, New York 10023

Distributed in the United Kingdom by
Hodder & Stoughton Services,
Po Box 6, Dunton Green,
Sevenoaks, Kent TN13 2XX.

An Arco Military Book

Published by the Prentice Hall Trade
Division

PRENTICE HALL PRESS and colophon
are registered trademarks of
Simon & Schuster Inc.

Originally published in 1983 in the United
Kingdom by Salamander Books Ltd.
Previously published in 1983 in the
United States by Arco Publishing, Inc.

Library of Congress Cataloging-in-
Publication Data

Jordan, John
    An illustrated guide to modern naval
    aviation and aircraft carriers

    (Illustrated military guides)
    "A Salamander book."
    1. Naval aviation. 2. Aircraft carriers
I. Title.   II. Series
VG90.J671983   358.4   83-2761

ISBN 0-668-05824-2

10 9 8 7 6 5 4 3 2

All correspondence concerning the
contents of this volume should be
addressed to Salamander Books Ltd.

Contents

Vessels and aircraft are arranged alphabetically by nation of origin
under three separate headings: air capable ships, shipborne
aviation and land-based aviation.

Credits

Author: John Jordan is a contributor to many important defence journals, a consultant to the Soviet section of 1980-81 "Jane's Fighting Ships", co-author of Salamander's "Balance of Military Power", and has written two companion "Guides", concerned with the modern US Navy and modern Soviet Navy.

Editor: Philip de Ste. Croix.
Designer: Roger Chesneau.

Line drawings (ships):
© John Jordan.
Line drawings (aircraft):
© Pilot Press Ltd.
Profile drawings:
© Salamander Books Ltd and Pilot Press Ltd.

Printed:
Henri Proost et Cie, Belgium.

Acknowledgments

Photographs: The publishers wish to thank all the official governmental archives, and warship and aircraft manufacturers who have supplied pictures for this book. Other photographs have been supplied by Austin Brown, Roger Chesneau and John Moore.

The Development of Naval Aviation

The two most important influences on carrier aviation in the immediate postwar period were the atomic bomb and jet aircraft. The atomic bomb, used only in the closing stages of the war against Japan, had serious implications for the future role of the aircraft carrier; indeed, there were many who felt that the operation of carrier task forces would be rendered impossible in the context of atomic warfare. Only the United Kingdom and the United States possessed carriers in 1945, and the state of the British economy in the immediate postwar period precluded new construction, so the Royal Navy had to be content to soldier on with its force of relatively small warbuilt carriers in the hope that funds would be forthcoming to complete at least some of the vessels already laid down.

The US Navy, on the other hand, saw the primacy of the carrier task forces built up during World War II threatened by new developments, and was determined to acquire its own strategic atomic role, operating heavy long-range bombers which could strike at targets well inland. These aircraft would be too large and too heavy to be operated by existing carriers, and new purpose-built ships would have to be designed to accommodate them. A large flush-decked carrier twice the displacement of the warbuilt Essex class, the *United States*, was proposed, and development of a new heavy bomber was begun. The US Navy's attempt to assume the strategic mantle led it into conflict with the US Air Force, which considered that the strategic mission would be best fulfilled by a large fleet of powerful intercontinental land-based bombers. The bitter arguments that ensued resulted in the cancellation of the new carrier, although development of the heavy bomber was continued; the latter was eventually to go into service as the A-3 Skywarrior. Only with American involvement in the Korean War of 1950-53 did the aircraft carrier come into its own again, proving its value in the conventional power projection role by mounting sustained air strikes in support of the troops ashore. With the additional defence funds released as a result of US involvement in this conflict the US Navy embarked on the construction of a new class of "super-carriers" derived from the *United States*. The massive increase in size represented by the Forrestal class was dictated by the requirement to operate the A-3 Skywarrior, which in turn owed its size to the requirement to carry a 12,000lb (5,450kg) atomic bomb — the minimum weight envisaged in the late 1940s. Ironically, by the time *Forrestal* was completed in 1955 the

Postwar

Top: The carrier *Monterey* (CVL 26) in 1944. The advent of jet-propelled aircraft in the immediate postwar period was to result in the demise of the axial flight deck.

Above: *Kitty Hawk* (CV 63) is typical of the US carrier as it evolved in the 1950s. She has a 10½° angled deck, four powerful steam catapults, and four deck edge lifts.

Left: The A-3 Skywarrior was designed to give the US Navy its own strategic nuclear strike capability. The dimensions of the postwar carriers were governed by the need to operate the A-3.

Above: HMS *Ark Royal* as completed, with a 5½° angled deck, steam catapults, and a deck edge lift (later removed).

minimum weight of nuclear bombs had been reduced to below 2,000lb (1,680lb, 760kg, for the Mk 7), and all existing fighter and light attack aircraft were being configured to carry them. The Forrestal design was therefore larger than it needed to be, even in the strategic strike role. However, as conventional aircraft grew bigger and bigger during the 1960s and 1970s, the benefits of "over-sizing" became more readily apparent, and all subsequent US carriers (10 to date) have been based on the *Forrestal*.

The development of jet aircraft, which were in their infancy in the late 1940s, had an equally dramatic effect on carrier design. Jets were sluggish at low speeds

Below: An F-4 Phantom catches the arrestor wires aboard the US carrier *Nimitz* (CVN 68). Modern carriers generally have four arrestor wires, which are stretched across the after section of the angled deck. Aircraft which fail to catch the wires simply lift off again and come round for a second attempt; axial-deck carriers needed safety barriers.

Right: A Phantom FG.1 of 892 NAS is stowed in the upper hangar of HMS *Ark Royal*. The Royal Navy was alone in persisting with the double hangar in the postwar period. The US Navy preferred the additional deck height conferred by a single hangar. On *Ark Royal* the aircraft lifts served both the upper and lower hangars.

and therefore required more powerful catapults than propeller-driven aircraft. Moreover, their much higher speed and notoriously high fuel consumption added up to low endurance and missions of short duration. The latter factor caused considerable disruption to the established deck-cycles for aircraft operation. Whereas in the Pacific War a carrier might take 45 minutes to an hour to recover the aircraft from a major strike, the total endurance of the early jets was only two hours, and this would also have to include the time taken to assemble aircraft above the ship and loiter time over the target or on patrol. This problem was aggravated by an axial flight deck layout which precluded simultaneous launch and landing operations.

The solutions to all these problems were provided not by the Americans but by the British, who were forced into a radical rethink of flight operations by the relatively small size of their carrier flight decks. The first steam catapult was installed experimentally in HMS *Perseus* in 1950. Even more important was the angled deck, which underwent trials aboard the US Essex-class

carrier *Antietam* in 1952, and was subsequently incorporated into the new Royal Navy carrier *Ark Royal* and the USS *Forrestal* while building. The angled deck made it possible to separate the take-off and landing areas of a carrier's flight deck, thus creating greater flexibility in operating cycles. It removed the need for crash barriers, which had always been a crude and potentially dangerous solution to the problem of aircraft missing the arrestor wires on landing, because aircraft could now abort the landing and come round again. The angled deck also created a triangular deck parking area to starboard on which aircraft could stand without interfering with take-off or landing operations. A third British invention, the mirror landing sight, helped the pilot to find the correct altitude and line of approach.

Within a few years these developments had been incorporated into every new carrier design, and had been retro-fitted in all but a few of the warbuilt vessels capable of being so modified. In the new carriers, the improved flight deck layout had important consequences for the arrangement of the aircraft lifts,

which as far as possible were kept clear of the angled deck, and were positioned in such a way as to serve the deck park and the forward catapults.

The late 1950s was a period of carrier proliferation, with new ships being laid down for the US Navy and the French Marine Nationale, and a number of the warbuilt light fleet carriers of the Royal Navy being purchased by the smaller navies and refitted to incorporate the latest developments.

Larger and Heavier Aircraft

The hopes of the smaller nations that they would be able to sustain attack carriers operating modern jet aircraft were relatively short-lived. Each new generation of jets was larger and heavier than its predecessor, and required more powerful catapults, greater lift capacity (and often size) and a stronger flight deck. This was particularly true of fleet air defence fighters, which were now expected to carry long-range air-to-air missiles and a fire control radar. In the Royal Navy the 15,000lb (6,800kg) Sea Venom of 1954 was succeeded by the 42,000lb (19,050kg) Sea Vixen of 1959, and ultimately by the 56,000lb (25,400kg) Phantom of 1966. By way of comparison, the French fleet carriers *Clemenceau* and *Foch* (completed in 1961 and 1963 respectively) had their catapults and lifts designed for a maximum capacity of 33,075lb (15,000kg).

The smaller powers soon fell by the wayside, and by the mid-1960s virtually all the former British light fleet carriers were operating a mix of A-4 Skyhawk light attack aircraft, S-2 Tracker or Alizé ASW aircraft, and antisubmarine helicopters. Even the Royal Navy was soon to succumb to the pressures generated by larger aircraft. Its only hope of staying the pace was a new generation of attack carriers of which the first, CVA-01, was due to be ordered in 1965. In the event CVA-01 was cancelled due to budgetary pressures, leaving *Ark Royal* as the only British carrier capable of operating modern aircraft. The Royal Navy subsequently turned its attention to the ASW stablemate of CVA-01, the Through Deck Cruiser (TDC), which would operate large antisubmarine helicopters. Outside the United States only the French persisted with the attack carrier, albeit at the cost of operating small and increasingly obsolescent aircraft from their decks.

Below: The F-8E Crusader, which is small by the standards of air defence fighters currently in service with the US Navy, is the largest aircraft to operate from the two French carriers in current service.

CARRIER AIR GROUPS (1967)

	Kitty Hawk (CVA) USA	Wasp (CVS) USA	Eagle UK	Clemenceau France	Melbourne Australia
All-Weather Fighters	24 F-4B Phantom		12 Sea Vixen FAW.1		
Day Fighters				10 F-8E Crusader	
All-Weather Attack	9 A-6A Intruder (+3 KA-3B)		10 Buccaneer S.2 (+4 Scimitar)		
Light Attack	28 A-4C Skyhawk			16 Etendard IVM	4 A-4G Skyhawk
Reconnaissance	6 RA-5C Vigilante			4 Etendard IVP	
Airborne Early Warning	4 E-2A Hawkeye	4 E-1B Tracer	4 Gannet AEW.3		
Antisubmarine Aircraft		20 S-2E Tracker		10 Alizé	6 S-2E Tracker
Antisubmarine Helicopters		16 SH-3A Sea King	8 Wessex HAS.1		10 Wessex HAS.31
TOTAL	**74 aircraft**	**40 aircraft**	**38 aircraft**	**40 aircraft**	**20 aircraft**

Above: The trend towards the diversification of carrier missions which we see in the navies of today was already well established by the mid-1960s. The Royal Navy was forced into a dramatic reduction in the number of strike aircraft which could be operated because of the relatively small size of its carriers. The small number of flight decks available also compelled the British to allocate valuable hangar space to a squadron of antisubmarine helicopters, whereas the US Navy of the 1960s was able to hive off the ASW mission to the older fleet carriers of the Essex class. The French resigned themselves to the operation of lighter, less capable fighters and strike aircraft, and dispensed with "extras" such as AEW aircraft; however, the French fleet carriers remain in commission. The Australian *Melbourne*, which is representative of the former British light fleet carriers in service with minor navies, shows the trend towards ASW operations in the smaller carrier: turbo-prop aircraft and helicopters do not require large flight decks and powerful catapults. Only the tiny A-4 Skyhawk is carried for self-defence. Nowadays, V/STOL offers the opportunity of seaborne strike from minimum decks.

ASW at Sea

Power projection was by no means the only mission of carrier aviation during the 1950s and 1960s. Even in the early postwar years the threat posed by Soviet submarines to Western control of the North Atlantic was readily apparent. Not only had the Soviets embarked on a massive programme of submarine construction, but they also had access to the latest German submarine technology, represented by the Type XXI, and the even more advanced Type XXVI with its Walter close-cycle propulsion system. Although in the event Soviet experiments with closed-cycle propulsion were to prove unsuccessful, the underwater problem was to be compounded by the development of nuclear-powered submarines, which entered service with the Soviet Navy in the late 1950s. These developments rendered existing antisubmarine technology obsolete; in particular, the speed advantage enjoyed by wartime escorts over their underwater prey had now virtually disappeared. The only possible solution lay in a combination of long-range underwater sensors and long-range stand-off weapons — homing torpedoes and ASW aircraft.

The US Navy, which ended World War II with a surplus of large flight decks, built up a force of ten hunter-killer groups each comprising an Essex-class carrier operating S-2 Tracker aircraft and HSS-1 ASW helicopters. The development of effective anti-submarine helicopters with dipping sonars, depth charges, and later sonobuoys and small homing torpedoes opened up new possibilities for navies with limited, or non-existent, carrier resources. Helicopters required no catapults or arrestor wires, just a small platform for take-off and landing and a hangar for maintenance; there was nothing to preclude their operation from cruisers, destroyers, or even frigates.

The Western European nations were foremost in promoting the small manned antisubmarine helicopter. In 1961 the Royal Navy began to complete a series of frigates operating the tiny Wasp helicopter. The Wasp differed from the larger carrier-borne ASW helicopters in that it carried no detection equipment and was therefore incapable of independent search operations. It was simply a delivery vehicle for Mk 44 torpedoes under control of its mother-ship. The French also experimented with small ASW helicopters at about this time, and eventually joined with the Royal Navy in the development of the Wasp's successor, the WG.13 Lynx. The Italians, who possessed no carriers of their own, displayed even greater commitment to the concept of the small manned ASW helicopter. The Bergamini-class frigates, the first of which

Above: The US Navy was a late runner in the manned helicopter stakes. The UH-2 Seasprite utility helicopter was chosen as the basis of the LAMPS I programme, becoming the SH-2D/F.

Left: A British Lynx, armed with two antisubmarine homing torpedoes, demonstrates its ability to remain operational even in the most extreme weather conditions. The grid in the flight deck is for the "Harpoon" securing system.

was completed in 1961 with a displacement of only 1,650 tons (full load), were the smallest ships of the period to operate a helicopter; and as early as 1958 construction had begun of two antisubmarine cruisers, *Andrea Doria* and *Caio Duilio*, which had a large hangar and flight deck aft for four Agusta-Bell 204 helicopters.

The US Navy was slow to develop small manned helicopters to operate from surface ships. Instead it chose to develop the DASH antisubmarine drone, a torpedo-delivery system controlled by the mother-ship. There was in any case some doubt as to the operational availability of small helicopters given the adverse weather conditions regularly encountered in the North Atlantic, and the US Navy preferred to rely on the ASROC missile. ASROC, however, had a range tailored to the 10,000yd (9,150m) maximum detection range of the SQS-23 sonar, and with the advent of the more powerful SQS-26, which offered the possibility of detection out to the first — or even the second — convergence zone (i.e. 30-60nm,

55.5 - 111km), a delivery system of much greater range was a pressing requirement. The DASH programme itself was something of a disaster, so the US Navy was compelled to turn to the manned helicopter in the early 1970s. The SH-2 Seasprite (LAMPS I) was larger than its European counterparts and carried sonobuoys, the data from which was analysed on board ship, in order to localise the contact.

The success of manned helicopter operations from antisubmarine vessels has been such that many of the latest destroyers and frigates — the US Navy's Spruance and FFG-7 classes, the British Type 22, the French Tourville and Georges Leygues classes, the Dutch and West German "Standaard" frigates — carry two helicopters to ensure maximum availability. The Canadians and Japanese have taken this a stage further by building large helicopter-carrying destroyers which can accommodate two or three of the large Sea King helicopters, which are capable of independent search and classification operations.

Left: Modern Italian frigates of the Lupo class (*Orsa* is depicted here) operate AB 212 helicopters for ASW, for surface strike, and to provide guidance for ship-launched SSMs.

Helicopters for Amphibious Assault

As early as the late 1940s the US Marine Corps initiated experiments in "vertical envelopment" amphibious assault techniques employing helicopters, and following the successful conversion in 1955 of a former escort carrier, *Thetis Bay*, the US Navy embarked upon the construction of purpose-built amphibious assault ships (LPHs) based on mercantile hulls. The Royal Navy was not slow to see the advantages of this form of amphibious assault, and duly converted two former light fleet carriers, *Bulwark* and *Albion*, as commando ships operating 16 Whirlwind (later Wessex) helicopters. The new French training ship *Jeanne d'Arc* was also configured to carry troops and to operate the large Super Frelon helicopter in this role in time of war. The withdrawal of the British from their East of Suez commitments in the late 1960s rendered the amphibious assault role less important to the Royal Navy, which failed to replace the Wessex with a more effective troop-carrying helicopter. The RN nevertheless retained a commando-carrying capability in its ASW carriers throughout the 1970s in order to bolster up NATO's Northern Flank, and this capability was greatly enhanced by the arrival of the Mk 4 Sea King in 1981. The Americans not only built large, heavy-lift helicopters such as the CH-46 Sea Knight and the even more powerful CH-53 Sea Stallion during this period, but in the late 1970s added the five massive assault ships of the Tarawa class to the seven LPHs of the Iwo Jima class.

The SCS and CV Concepts

With the ageing ASW carriers of the Essex class in urgent need of replacement in the early 1970s, the US Navy proposed a new purpose-built utility design designated the Sea Control Ship (SCS). The latter would operate 14 SH-3 Sea King ASW helicopters and a detachment of 3 AV-8 Harrier V/STOL fighters for self-defence. The design was eventually branded too austere and was discarded, but the ASW capabilities of the big fleet carriers were greatly enhanced by embarking a squadron of S-3 Viking fixed-wing aircraft and a squadron of SH-3 Sea Kings; the designation of the carriers was changed from CVA to CV.

Land-Based ASW

Long-range maritime patrol (LRMP) aircraft had established their value in World War II during the later stages of the German submarine offensive in the North Atlantic. Large bomber-type aircraft fitted with surface search radars and magnetic anomaly detectors (MAD), and armed with depth charges, continued to serve in this role with the NATO powers throughout the 1950s, the principal aircraft being the American P-2 Neptune and the British Shackleton. These aircraft were intended to catch unsuspecting diesel-powered submarines on the surface, or at least to force them to remain submerged, draining the power from their batteries. The advent of the true submarine, with nuclear propulsion, threatened to make LRMP aircraft obsolete. However, the development of broad-area surveillance systems, such as the American SOSUS, was to revolutionise ocean ASW operations and re-establish the importance of land-based patrol aircraft. The success of the new tactics was such that it resulted in the demise of the carrier-based hunter-killer groups favoured by NATO during the 1950s and the early 1960s. By the late 1960s, for example, both Canada and the Netherlands had discarded their ex-British light fleet carriers in favour of LRMP aircraft. Similar arguments may have influenced the US Navy's decision not to proceed with the SCS, and they undoubtedly formed the basis of the decision (since rescinded) in the British White Paper of 1981 to dispense with one of the three Invincible-class ASW carriers, retaining only *Illustrious* and *Ark Royal*.

Left: Royal Marines embark on a Wessex HU.5 assault helicopter during a NATO exercise.

Below left: RH-53 Sea Stallion helicopter such as was used for the ill-fated attempt to rescue hostages from Iran.

Below: A P-2 Neptune of the US Navy. The Neptune was the major Western ASW patrol aircraft of the 1950s, but it has now been replaced by the more advanced P-3 Orion, and only the Japanese P-2J model is still in first-line service.

Right: Two US Navy S-3A Viking antisubmarine patrol aircraft in company with an SH-3 Sea King and an E-2C Hawkeye. The Viking has added a new dimension to the carrier air wings.

The basic principle of ocean ASW operations employing broad area underwater surveillance is that submarines detected at long range by the use of passive hydrophones located on the seabed, or by the deployment of passive arrays towed by surface vessels, are "pounced on" by LRMP aircraft either on patrol or "scrambled" from the nearest air base. The aircraft then attempts to localise the contact with sonobuoys and MAD and makes its attack with homing torpedoes or depth charges. Operators at consoles on board the aircraft process and monitor the data from the sonobuoys and direct the attack. The current standard NATO aircraft flying this mission is the P-3 Orion, backed up by the British Nimrod and the French Atlantic. The sophisticated carrier-borne S-3 Viking is also capable of employment in conjunction with SOSUS or towed arrays.

Maritime Strike
A number of European nations operate squadrons of land-based aircraft whose primary mission is maritime strike. Generally speaking, these are countries which have never possessed carriers,

like the Federal Republic of Germany, or countries which have abandoned the attack carrier, like the United Kingdom. Several NATO countries operate the F-104 Starfighter (being replaced by the Tornado in the FRG) in this role; the RAF operates ex-Fleet Air Arm Buccaneers from bases in the UK.

Soviet Naval Aviation
Although certainly influenced by developments in naval aviation which took place in the West in the 1950s and 1960s, the Soviet Navy, which was concerned with defending the territorial integrity of the USSR and not with controlling the sea lanes, took a very different course. In order to counter the NATO carrier task forces a large force of land-based bombers, armed with stand-off anti-ship missiles, was built up in the late 1950s and early 1960s. Ocean surveillance and targeting data would be provided by the Tu-20 Bear D, which was converted from a strategic Air Force bomber. With the more recent addition of the formidable Tu-26 Backfire bomber, this force remains the cornerstone of Soviet anti-carrier strategy, particularly in the seas adjacent to the Soviet Union.

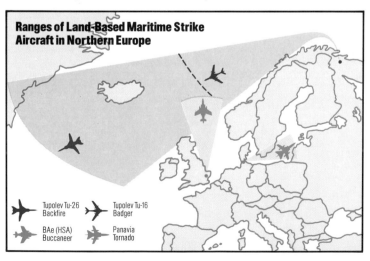

Ranges of Land-Based Maritime Strike Aircraft in Northern Europe

Tupolev Tu-26 Backfire
Tupolev Tu-16 Badger
BAe (HSA) Buccaneer
Panavia Tornado

Soviet interest in ASW began only in the early 1960s, when US Navy Polaris submarines began their patrols in the Mediterranean and the Norwegian Seas. The development of ASW patrol aircraft such as the Il-38 May was undertaken, and the influence of the West European NATO powers (especially Italy and France) was apparent in the design of two large antisubmarine cruisers for SSBN hunting operations in the Eastern Mediterranean. The Moskva class, which operated the intermediate-sized Ka-25 Hormone helicopter, was succeeded after a break of several years by the Kiev class, which embarked a squadron of Yak-36 Forger VTOL fighter-bombers in addition to their ASW helicopter squadron. The Ka-25 Hormone was also embarked on a series of Large Antisubmarine Ships (BPKs) completed from 1970 onwards. The latest of these, the Udaloy class, can accommodate two helicopters of an improved type (the Ka-32 Helix) — a development which parallels current practice in the West.

Left: A map of Northern Europe showing the approximate operational radii of the various maritime strike aircraft.

Below: New Soviet carrier/cruiser *Novorossisk*, with HMS *Illustrious*.

Air-Capable Ships

25 de Mayo

Completed: 1945.
Names: V 2 *25 de Mayo*.
Displacement: 15,892 tons standard; 19,896 tons full load.
Dimensions: Length overall 698ft (212·7m); beam 138ft (42·1m); draught 25ft (7·6m).
Elevators: 2 centre-line, 45ft x 34ft (13·7m x 10·4m).
Catapults: 1 steam.
Propulsion: 2-shaft geared steam turbines; 40,000shp = 24·5kt.
Armament: 9 40mm AA (9 x 1).
Aircraft: 10 Super Etendard; 5 S-2E Tracker; 4 SH-3D Sea King.
Complement: 1,509.

Formerly the British light fleet carrier *Venerable*, this vessel was purchased by the Netherlands Navy in 1948 and renamed *Karel Doorman*. She subsequently underwent an extensive modernisation 1955-58, when she was given an

Right: A 1980 view of *25 de Mayo* following the removal of part of the original radar outfit and the extension of the flight deck abaft the island. *25 de Mayo* accompanied the Argentine invasion force which undertook the initial occupation of the Falklands in April 1982, but was apparently prevented from taking a more active part in the conflict by problems with her single catapult. She would, of course, have been a prime target.

This section of the book covers all vessels whose primary function is the operation of fixed- or rotary-wing aircraft. Large helicopter destroyers (DDH) are included, but not antisubmarine frigates or amphibious vessels such as dock landing ships (LPD).

angled deck, a single steam catapult forward, and a mirror landing sight. The island was completely rebuilt to accommodate an outfit of Dutch radars, and an armament of 40mm single AA guns was fitted. After modernisation she operated first as an attack carrier, with Sea Hawk fighter-bombers and TBM-3 Avengers, then as an ASW carrier with S-2 Tracker aircraft and HSS-1 (SH-34) Seabat helicopters. In 1965-66 she was reboilered using boilers from the uncompleted British *Leviathan* of the same class. She was badly damaged by a boiler-room fire in 1968, and was subsequently sold to Argentina. She was refitted in the Netherlands before being handed over in 1969, and in the early 1970s a British CAAIS data system compatible with the ADAWS-4 system of the two Type 42 destroyers ordered in 1970 was installed. The air group of the ship during the 1970s comprised A-4 Skyhawks, S-2 Trackers and SH-3 Sea Kings. In a 1980 refit the flight deck was enlarged abaft the island to permit parking of three additional aircraft, and 14 Super Etendard fighter-bombers were ordered from France to replace the A-4 Skyhawks. Only five of these had been delivered before the Falklands conflict of 1982, and they were operated from land bases during this time. Problems with her catapult apparently hampered her participation in the campaign.

Left: A Super Etendard of the Argentine Navy. Fourteen aircraft of this type were ordered from France to replace the A-4Q Skyhawk. Although five had been delivered by April 1982 *25 de Mayo* had not yet been fitted with the necessary electronics, and the Super Etendards were operated from the southern air base of Río Grande. From there they carried out a series of devastating strikes on the British task force. Armed with AM-39 Exocet ASMs they hit first the destroyer *Sheffield,* then the container ship *Atlantic Conveyor;* both vessels were severely damaged, were abandoned, and subsequently sank.

BRAZIL
Minas Gerais

Completed: 1945.
Names: A 11 *Minas Gerais*.
Displacement: 15,890 tons standard; 19,890 tons full load.
Dimensions: Length overall 695ft (211·8m); beam 119ft (36·3m); draught 25ft (7·6m).
Elevators: 2 centre-line, 45ft x 34ft (13·7m x 10·4m).
Catapults: 1 steam.
Propulsion: 2-shaft geared steam turbines; 40,000shp = 24kt.
Armament: 10 40mm AA (2 x 4, 1 x 2).
Aircraft: 8 S-2E Tracker; 4 SH-3D Sea King, 2 Bell 206B; 2 SA.530 Ecureuil.
Complement: 1,300.

Completed as the British light fleet carrier *Vengeance,* this vessel was purchased by Brazil in 1956 and refitted in Rotterdam. She emerged in 1960 with a flight deck angled at fully 8·5 degrees, a steam catapult, US radars and two new aircraft lifts. The catapult can launch aircraft weighing 30,000lb (13,640kg). In a refit 1976-81 a data link compatible with the data system of the large Niteroi-class ASW frigates was installed. Throughout her operational life *Minas Gerais* has served as an ASW carrier, with S-2 Tracker aircraft and helicopters: first the HSS-1 (SH-34) Seabat, then the larger SH-3 Sea King.

Right: *Minas Gerais*, with standard US Navy-pattern deck markings. She retains a single catapult in order to operate her S-2E Trackers, one of which is seen here on deck.

CANADA
Iroquois

Completed: 1972-73.
Names: DDH 280 *Iroquois*; DDH 281 *Huron*; DDH 282 *Athabascan*; DDH 283 *Algonquin.*
Displacement: 3,551 tons standard; 4,200 tons full load.
Dimensions: Length overall 426ft (129·8m); beam 50ft (15·2m); draught 14ft 6in (4·4m).
Elevators: None.
Catapults: None.
Propulsion: 2-shaft COGOG; 2 Pratt & Whitney FT4A2 gas-turbines, 50,000bhp = 29kt; 2 Pratt & Whitney FT12 AH3 gas-turbines, 7,400bhp for cruising.

Right: The Canadian destroyer *Iroquois* (DDH 280). The forward superstructure incorporates the bridge and the command spaces, but the after part of the ship is dominated by the large double hangar and flight deck for two Sea King ASW helicopters. The twin funnels are canted outwards in order to keep the hot exhaust gases from the gas-turbines clear of the electronic equipment. The Sea Sparrow magazine and handling arrangements are immediately forward of the bridge structure. The Iroquois class ships are very capable, if expensive.

Armament: 1 single 5in (127mm) OTO Melara Compact gun; 2 Sea Sparrow launchers (2 x 4, + 24 reloads); 2 triple Mk 32 ASW TT; 1 triple Limbo A/S mortar.
Aircraft: 2 CH-124 Sea King.
Complement: 285.

Latest in a series of large anti-submarine escorts built by Canada in the postwar period, the Iroquois class is essentially a platform for two large CH-124 Sea King helicopters, which are accommodated in a large double hangar aft and can be operated even in heavy weather thanks to their Beartrap haul-down and securing system. *Iroquois* is also noteworthy for being the first major Western warship with all-gas turbine propulsion. A follow-up class of 20 helicopter destroyers of a new design has for long been projected, but it is uncertain whether any will be built.

FRANCE

Clemenceau

Completed: 1961-63.
Names: R 98 *Clemenceau*; R 99 *Foch*.
Displacement: 22,000 tons standard; 32,780 tons full load.
Dimensions: Length overall 870ft (265m); beam 168ft (51·2m); draught 28ft 2in (8·6m).
Elevators: 1 inboard (fwd), 56ft x 43ft (17m x 13m); 1 deck edge (aft), 52ft x 36ft (16m x 11m); each 44,000lb (20,000kg) capacity.
Catapults: 2 Mitchell-Brown steam.
Propulsion: 2-shaft geared steam turbines; 126,000shp = 32kt.
Armament: 8 single 100mm D-P guns.
Aircraft: 16 Super Etendard; 3 Etendard IVP; 10 F-8E Crusader; 7 Alizé, 2 Alouette III.
Complement: 1,338.

These two light fleet carriers were laid down in the mid-1950s, and incorporated all the major advances made in carrier operation during the immediate postwar period. The flight deck measures 543ft (165·5m) by 97ft (29·5m) and is angled at 8 degrees to the ship's axis. The forward aircraft lift is

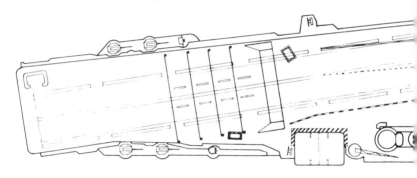

offset to starboard with one of the two 170ft 7in (52m) catapults to port; the second catapult is located on the angled deck. The after lift is positioned on the deck edge to clear the flight deck and to increase hangar capacity. The hangar, which is offset to port, has a usable length of 499ft (152m) and a width of 72-79ft (22-24m), with 23ft (7m) clearance overhead.

A new generation of aircraft was designed to operate from these carriers. Two flights each of 10 Etendard IVM/P ground support fighters (with integral reconnaissance aircraft) were initially embarked, together with a flight of Alizé turbo-prop ASW aircraft; F-8E Crusaders were purchased from the USA in 1963 and from 1966 made up the interceptor flight. The Etendard IVM has recently been replaced by the Super Etendard, which can carry anti-ship missiles (ASM) and has a nuclear strike capability, but the small size and light construction of the ships, together with the limited capacity (20 tonnes) of their lifts and catapults, has made it difficult to find a suitable replacement for the Crusader. A further limitation on the effectiveness of these ships is the absence of integral airborne early warning (AEW).

Clemenceau and *Foch* have recently been refitted with SENIT 2 tactical data systems. Both ships have served in the Mediterranean since 1975, when they transferred from the Atlantic. It is envisaged that they will be replaced by two nuclear-powered vessels of similar size in the 1990s.

Below: A plan view of *Clemenceau*. Note the lift arrangement.

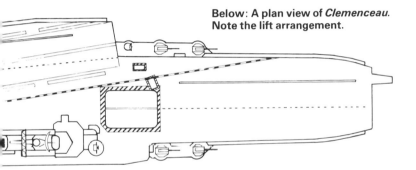

Left: A recent view of *Clemenceau*, with new deck markings. She and her sister *Foch* now alternate in the attack carrier role, the other vessel having an air complement weighted towards ASW, with strike fighters and rotary- and fixed-wing antisubmarine aircraft. *Clemenceau* is operating here in the attack carrier role. There are eight of the new Super Etendard strike fighters forward, together with a single F-8E(FN) Crusader interceptor. Five more Super Etendards are parked amidships, together with a second Crusader, and an Alizé ASW aircraft can be seen farther aft. These two ships will be succeeded in service by a pair of nuclear-powered carriers, authorised in 1980.

FRANCE
Jeanne d'Arc

Completed: 1964.
Names: R 97 *Jeanne d'Arc*.
Displacement: 10,000 tons standard; 12,365 tons full-load.
Dimensions: Length overall 597ft (182m); beam 79ft (24m); draught 24ft (7·3m).
Elevators: 1 stern, 59ft x 28ft (18m x 8·5m), 26,450lb (12,000kg) capacity.
Catapults: None.
Propulsion: 2-shaft geared steam turbines; 40,000shp = 26·5kt.
Armament: 6 MM 38 Exocet SSMs; 4 single 100mm D-P guns.
Aircraft: 4/8 Super Frelon (see text).
Complement: 617 (inc. 183 officer cadets).

The helicopter cruiser *Jeanne d'Arc* serves in peacetime as a training ship, with berths for 183 officer cadets. In wartime she could be employed either as an ASW helicopter carrier, or as an assault ship with accommodation for a battalion of 700 troops.

The hull-form was based on that of the anti-aircraft cruiser *Colbert*. A conventional cruiser superstructure forward accommodates the boiler uptakes, the surveillance radars, much of the ship's armament, an action information centre, and a control centre for amphibious landing operations. The after part of the ship is dominated by a helicopter deck 203ft by 69ft (62m x 21m) with a hangar beneath. The single centre-line lift is integrated into the after end of the flight deck, with aviation workshops to the sides. The hangar was designed to accommodate four large Super Frelon helicopters, although in her role as a training ship *Jeanne d'Arc* generally operates smaller helicopters such as the Alouette III and the WG.13 Lynx. In wartime hangar space could be doubled by removing some of the officer cadet accommodation. Five helicopter spots are marked out on the flight deck, and two simultaneous take-offs are possible.

In 1974 *Jeanne d'Arc* had six box launchers for MM 38 Exocet SSMs fitted forward of the bridge. It is envisaged that the Crotale SAM system will be fitted in the near future.

Left: The helicopter carrier *Jeanne d'Arc* comes alongside for a five-day visit to San Francisco in 1971. In peacetime she is employed as a training ship, and undertakes regular round-the-world cruises. Note the single 100mm guns aft.

Below: *Jeanne d'Arc* is seen here operating two large Super Frelon antisubmarine helicopters from her flight deck. Six launchers for Exocet anti-ship missiles were fitted forward of the super-structure in 1974, giving the ship a greater capability.

INDIA
Vikrant

Completed: 1961.
Names: R 11 *Vikrant*.
Displacement: 15,700 tons standard; 19,500 tons full load.
Dimensions: Length overall 700ft (213·4m); beam 128ft (39m); draught 24ft (7·3m).
Elevators: 2 centre-line, 45ft x 34ft (13·7m x 10·4m).
Catapults: 1 steam.
Propulsion: 2-shaft geared steam turbines; 40,000shp = 24kt.
Armament: 15 40mm AA (4 x 2, 7 x 1).
Aircraft: 16 Sea Hawk; 4 Alizé (see text).
Complement: 1,340.

Laid down as the British light fleet carrier *Hercules*, this vessel was incomplete when purchased by India in 1957. An angled deck was fitted, together with a steam catapult and mirror landing sight, before *Vikrant* was finally handed over in 1961. She was partially air-conditioned and, as insulation for the tropical climate in which she would operate, the ship's sides were sprayed with asbestos cement. The hangar, which is centrally located with the two aircraft lifts at either end, is 445ft long and 52ft wide (135·6m x 15·8m).

From her completion *Vikrant* has served as an attack carrier, operating Sea Hawk jet fighter-bombers and a handful of Alizé turbo-prop ASW aircraft. In 1979 she was taken in hand for a major modernisation which included the replacement of boilers and engines and the installation of new sensors and a combat information centre. She will de-commission again in mid-1983 when a "ski jump" will be constructed for the Sea Harrier aircraft ordered as replacements for the Sea Hawk. Six Sea Harriers are on order, and as construction of the ski jump will involve removal of the catapult it seems likely that the elderly Alizé ASW aircraft will be discarded in favour of Sea King and Alouette III helicopters. After reconstruction *Vikrant* is scheduled to remain in service for a further ten years.

Above: A Sea Harrier FRS.51 in the colours of the Indian Navy. Six FRS.51 single-seat fighters plus two T.60 two-seat trainers have been ordered from the UK to operate from the carrier *Vikrant*. They will replace the ancient Sea Hawk fighter-bombers which have been in service since the ship first commissioned in the early 1960s.

Below: The carrier *Vikrant* entering Grand Harbour, Malta, during the early part of her career. Eight Sea Hawk fighter-bombers are parked amidships, and four French Alizé ASW aircraft are parked aft. *Vikrant* is now receiving a major modernisation which includes the fitting of a "ski-jump".

Giuseppe Garibaldi

Completed: (1985).
Names: C 551 *Giuseppe Garibaldi* (building).
Displacement: 10,043 tons standard; 13,370 tons full load.
Dimensions: Length overall 591ft (180·1); beam 100ft (30·5m); draught 22ft (6·7m).
Elevators: 2 inboard, 59ft x 34ft (18m x 10·4m).
Catapults: None.
Propulsion: 2-shaft COGAG; 4 LM2500 gas-turbines; 80,000bhp = 29kt.
Armament: 4 Otomat Mk 2 SSMs; 2 Albatros SAM systems (2 x 8); 3 twin Breda 40mm AA; 2 triple Mk 32 ASW TT.
Aircraft: 12 SH-3D Sea King.
Complement: 560 (825 max.).

Garibaldi is the first purpose-built through-deck carrier to be laid down for the Italian navy. She is designed exclusively for antisubmarine operations, operating the big SH-3D Sea King in place of the AB 204/212 helicopters operated by previous Italian ASW cruisers. The hangar, which is located

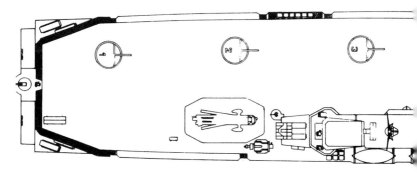

Below: A model of *Giuseppe Garibaldi* with five SH-3D Sea Kings on deck and a sixth in the process of being struck down on the forward lift. It now

centrally, is 361ft (110m) long and 20ft (6m) high, and has a maximum width of 49ft (15m); the centre section, which as in the British *Invincible* has large gas-turbine uptakes to starboard, is somewhat narrower. A maximum of twelve Sea Kings can be struck down in the hangar, which is divided into three sections by fire curtains. An alternative loading of ten Sea Harriers is possible, but the Italian government has so far shown a marked reluctance to purchase this aircraft on political and economic grounds. The hexagonal lifts are offset to starboard fore and aft of the massive island. Six helicopter spots are marked out on the flight deck.

Only short-range air defence and close-in anti-missile systems are to be fitted and these are all of Italian design and manufacture, as are the Selenia surveillance, 3-D tracking and fire control radars. A bow sonar of US manufacture is fitted, and the computerised data system will be capable of handling 200 target tracks.

The ordering of *Garibaldi* was delayed by financial difficulties, and the design has undergone a number of modifications since the ship was initially conceived. She was finally laid down in March 1981 and when compeleted she will replace the two ASW cruisers of the Andrea Doria class.

Below: A plan view of *Giuseppe Garibaldi*. Note the large island.

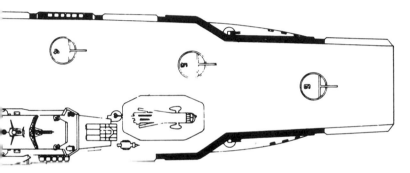

appears that *Garibaldi* will be given a low-angle "ski jump" for V/STOL aircraft. The carrier was launched in June 1983.

Vittorio Veneto

Completed: 1969.
Names: C 550 *Vittorio Veneto*.
Displacement: 7,500 tons standard; 8,870 tons full load.
Dimensions: Length overall 589ft (179·5m); beam 64ft (19·5m); draught 20ft (6m).
Elevators: 1 centre-line, 51ft x 26ft (15·5m x 8m).
Catapults: None.
Propulsion: 2-shaft geared steam turbines; 73,000shp = 30·5kt.
Armament: Twin Mk 10 launcher (60 Terrier/ASROC missiles); 8 single 76mm D-P guns (see text); 2 triple Mk 32 ASW TT.
Aircraft: 9 AB 212 or 4 SH-3D Sea King.
Complement: 565.

Vittorio Veneto was the third ship in a series of air-capable cruisers completed by the Italians in the 1960s. The earlier *Andrea Doria* and *Caio Duilio* were smaller, could operate only four AB 204 ASW helicopters, and had conventional helicopter-handling arrangements comprising a large double hangar incorporated into the after superstructure leading directly onto a flight deck above the stern. In *Vittorio Veneto* these arrangements were considerably modified; there is an extra deck aft, beneath which a hangar 90ft

by 50ft (27·4m x 15·2m) is located. Four helicopter spots are marked out on the capacious flight deck, and the latter is served by a single large centre-line lift immediately aft of the superstructure. Two sets of fin-stabilisers result in a steady platform for helicopter operations. *Vittorio Veneto* was designed to operate nine AB 204 ASW helicopters, all of which could be accommodated in the hangar. These have now been superseded by the improved AB 212, with an alternative complement of four Sea Kings. The hangar, which is only two decks high, cannot accommodate the latter, which therefore have to remain on deck.

As completed *Vittorio Veneto* had a "cruiser" armament similar to that of the Doria class, with a Mk 10 twin SAM launcher forward and single 76mm guns disposed in symmetrical fashion around the superstructure. She is currently undergoing an extensive modernisation in which the Terrier system will be upgraded to fire the Standard SM-1 (ER) missile, and the single 76mm will be replaced by three twin 40mm/70 Breda compact mountings with Dardo fire control systems. Four Otomat Mk 2 SSMs will also be fitted.

Below: The helicopter cruiser *Vittorio Veneto* is seen here before her recent refit, with the original air defence armament of US Terrier missiles and eight single 76mm AA guns. The five small helo circles aft are for AB 212 ASW helicopters, of which she carries nine in a large hangar beneath the flight deck. The lift is concealed by the superstructure. *Vittorio Veneto*'s limited capacity has prompted the building of *Garibaldi*.

Haruna and Shirane

Completed: 1973-74/1980-81.
Names: 141 *Haruna;* 142 *Hiei.*
143 *Shirane;* 144 *Kurama.*
Displacement: 4,700/5,200 tons standard; 6,300/6,800 tons full load.
Dimensions: Length overall 502ft/521ft (153m/158·8m); beam 57ft 5in
(17·5m); draught 16ft 9in/17ft 5in (5·1m/5·3m).
Elevators: None.
Catapults: None.
Propulsion: 2-shaft geared steam turbines; 70,000shp = 32kt.
Armament: ASROC launcher Mk 16 (1 x 8); 2 single 5in (127mm) Mk 42 guns;
2 triple Mk 32 ASW TT; (Shirane class only) Sea Sparrow BPDMS launcher Mk
25 (1 x 8); 2 Phalanx CIWS.
Aircraft: 3 SH-3B Sea King.
Complement: 340/370.

Japan's constitution forbids the maintenance of armed forces for aggressive
intent. The Japanese Maritime Self-Defense Force (JMSDF) is therefore
tasked with purely defensive missions, the foremost being the protection of
the sea lanes around Japan, which are essential to her economy. The naval
force built up since the late 1950s has therefore been oriented towards
antisubmarine warfare, employing weapons and helicopters of US origin. The
largest vessels of the JMSDF are four helicopter-carrying destroyers of the
Haruna and *Shirane* classes. The former two ships were completed in 1973-
74, and the second pair 1980-81.

Both classes have a double helicopter hangar for three large SH-3 Sea King
helicopters integrated into the superstructure. The flight deck extends to the
stern and incorporates the Canadian Beartrap haul-down system. The funnel
arrangement reflects the internal layout of the hangar, the single funnel of

**Below: The destroyer *Shirane* incorporates a number of improvements
over the earlier two vessels, particularly with regard to air defence
capabilities. A Sea King is landing on.**

Above: *Haruna*, the first in a series of large helicopter-carrying destroyers built for the JMSDF.

Haruna being offset to port and the after funnel of *Shirane*, which has separate boiler rooms on echelon, to starboard. There is an ASROC launcher forward of the bridge and Mk 32 torpedo tubes abreast the superstructure. Hull sonars of Japanese manufacture are fitted, and the Shirane class also has the SQS-35 variable depth sonar, and an SQR-18 TACTASS towed array. Two quick-firing 5-inch (127mm) Mk 42 guns are mounted for air defence in all four units, and these are complemented by BPDMS missile and Phalanx CIWS systems in *Shirane* and *Kurama*. The earlier two ships are to be retro-fitted with these systems and the SQS-35 VDS, and all four ships will receive Harpoon SSMs.

Dédalo

Completed: 1943.
Names: R 01 *Dédalo*.
Displacement: 13,000 tons standard; 16,416 tons full load.
Dimensions: Length overall 622ft 6in (189·7m); beam 109ft 2in (33·3m); draught 26ft 7in (8·1m).
Elevators: 2 centre-line, 44ft x 42ft (13·4m x 12·8m).
Catapults: None.
Propulsion: 4-shaft geared steam turbines; 100,000shp = 31kt.
Armament: 22 40mm (1 x 4, 9 x 2).
Aircraft: 5 AV-8S Matador; 8 SH-3D Sea King; 4 AB 212ASW.
Complement: 1,100 (+ air group).

In 1967 the former US Navy aviation transport *Cabot*, refitted as an ASW helicopter carrier, was transferred to Spain for a period of five years. She was purchased outright in 1973, and since 1976 has operated AV-8S Harrier V/STOL aircraft (re-christened "Matador" in Spanish service) in addition to her antisubmarine helicopters. *Dédalo* is currently flagship of the Spanish fleet; she will be replaced by the new purpose-built *Príncipe de Asturias*

Right: The carrier *Dédalo*, flagship of the Spanish Navy. Although obsolete by the standards of other major navies, this elderly ex-US Navy vessel has provided invaluable experience in the operation of both rotary- and fixed-wing (V/STOL) aircraft. Three Sea Kings can be seen on deck in this view.

Príncipe de Asturias

Completed: (1985).
Names: R 11 *Príncipe de Asturias*.
Displacement: 14,500 tons full load.
Dimensions: Length overall 640ft (195·1m); beam 98ft 5in (30m); draught 22ft (6·7m).
Elevators: 1 inboard, 1 stern.
Catapults: None.
Propulsion: 1-shaft COGAG; 2 LM2500 gas-turbines; 46,600bhp = 26kt.
Armament: 4 Meroka CIWS.

Below: The hull of Spain's new carrier, *Príncipe de Asturias*, is launched ready for fitting out. She has a "ski jump" incorporated in the bow for operations with the Matador.

Aircraft: 6/8 AV-8S Matador; 6/8 SH-3D Sea King; 8/4 VERTREP helicopters.
Complement: 791.

Príncipe de Asturias is under construction as a replacement for the old carrier *Dédalo*. The design is based on that of the ill-fated Sea Control Ship (SCS) proposed by the US Navy in the early 1970s for antisubmarine and air superiority missions in low-threat areas. An austere design with a single-shaft propulsion system and minimal electronics, the SCS is built around its aviation facilities, which include a full-width hangar occupying the after two thirds of the ship. Modifications incorporated in the Spanish vessel include a 12-degree ski jump and the Spanish Meroka 20mm CIWS. *Príncipe de Asturias* was ordered in 1977, laid down in 1979 and launched in May 1982.

UK
Invincible

Completed: 1980 onwards.
Names: R 05 *Invincible*; R 06 *Illustrious;* R 07 *Ark Royal* (building).
Displacement: 16,256 tons standard; 19,812 tons full load.
Dimensions: Length overall 677ft (206·3m); beam 105ft (32m); draught 21ft (6·4m).
Elevators: 2 inboard, 55ft x 32ft (16·8m x 9·7m).
Catapults: None.
Propulsion: 2-shaft COGAG; 4 Olympus TM3B gas-turbines; 112,000bhp = 28kt.
Armament: Twin Sea Dart launcher (22 missiles); 2 Phalanx CIWS.
Aircraft: 5 Sea Harrier FRS.1; 9 Sea King HAS.5; 2 Sea King AEW.
Complement: 1,000 + 320 (air group).

Following the decision taken in the mid-1960s not to proceed with a new generation of attack carriers for the Royal Navy, design work commenced on a large air-capable antisubmarine command cruiser (designated Through Deck Cruiser, or TDC) for deployment within the NATO Eastlant area of operations. The ship was originally to operate only large ASW helicopters, but at a relatively late stage in the design process provision was made for operating Sea Harrier V/STOL aircraft, which would have the task of intercepting hostile reconnaissance and antisubmarine patrol aircraft. A final amendment made in 1976-77 established a requirement for the ship to double as a commando carrier. In recognition of the new capabilities conferred on them by their complement of fixed-wing aircraft the ships were redesignated "ASW aircraft carriers" in 1980.

The hangar has a "dumb-bell" shape, with a narrow centre section and large bays at either end. This arrangement was dictated by the provision of large exhaust uptakes for the gas-turbines to starboard, but was not regarded as a serious problem when it was envisaged that only helicopters would be operated; it nevertheless imposes some constraints on the movement of fixed-wing aircraft at hangar level. The McTaggart Scott lifts are of a novel design, employing a hydraulic "scissors" mechanism in place of the customary wires and pulleys; this arrangement enables the lifts to load from all four sides, whereas conventional lifts load from one or two sides only.

Unlike earlier Royal Navy carriers the Invincible class have an open forecastle. The flight deck, which is 600ft long and 44ft wide (182·9m x 13·4m), is offset to port and angled slightly in order to clear the Sea Dart launcher, which occupies a fairly central position on the forecastle. *Invincible* and *Illustrious* have a 7-degree "ski jump" at the forward end of the flight deck ▶

Right: The antisubmarine carrier *Invincible* on sea trials in 1979. Originating from the "Through Deck Cruiser" proposal of the late 1960s, the class incorporates its own area defence system in the form of the Sea Dart missile.

Below: A plan view of *Invincible* as first completed.

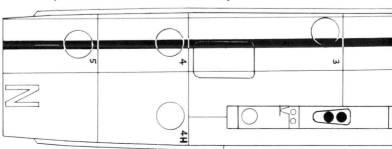

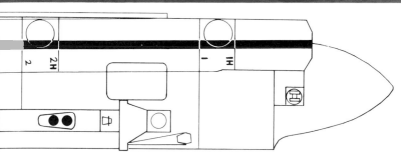

to assist short rolling take-offs by the Sea Harrier. The payload of the latter is increased by 1,500lb (680kg) if it uses the ski jump. The ski jump fitted to *Ark Royal* will be angled at fully 12 degrees, and will necessitate the repositioning of the Sea Dart launcher. As a result of experience in the Falklands conflict American Vulcan/Phalanx close-in defence weapons have been purchased for *Invincible* and *Illustrious*. One Phalanx CIWS has now been installed alongside the Sea Dart launcher, and a second is fitted at the after end of the flight deck on the starboard side.

The planned peacetime complement of aircraft has recently been boosted by the addition of two Sea King AEW helicopters as a result of experience in the Falklands. During the latter conflict *Invincible* operated between eight and twelve Sea Harriers in addition to her squadron of Mk 5 Sea Kings. Her sister *Illustrious*, which relieved her in the summer of 1982, operated ten Sea Harriers while on patrol in the South Atlantic. The limited capacity of the hangar means that a permanent deck-park has to be employed in order to accommodate such a large complement of aircraft.

For the NATO Eastlant role which constitutes their primary mission *Invincible* and her sisters are equipped with a sophisticated antisubmarine command centre and first-rate communications. They are also fitted with a Type 184 hull sonar. In early 1982 a contract was signed with the Australian government for the sale of *Invincible*, but following the Falklands conflict this agreement was rescinded, and it is now envisaged that all three carriers will continue in service with the Royal Navy. *Ark Royal* is due to enter service in 1986.

Above: *Illustrious* passes *Ark Royal* (still fitting out) on the River Tyne in 1982.

Below: *Invincible* with five Sea Harriers of 801 NAS aboard in early 1982.

UK
Hermes

Completed: 1959.
Names: R 12 *Hermes*.
Displacement: 23,900 tons standard; 28,700 tons full load.
Dimensions: Length overall 744ft (226·8m); beam 151ft (46m); draught 29ft (8·8m).
Elevators: 1 deck edge (fwd), 54ft x 36ft (16·5m x 11m); 1 centre-line (aft), 54ft x 44ft (16·5m x 13·4m).
Catapults: None.
Propulsion: 2-shaft geared steam turbines, 76,000shp = 28kt.
Armament: 2 quadruple launchers for Seacat missiles.
Aircraft: 5 Sea Harrier FRS.1; 9-12 Sea King HAS.5/HC.4; 2 Sea King AEW.
Complement: 1,170 + 350 (air group).

Laid down in 1944 as a light fleet carrier, *Hermes* was not completed until 1959. The delay resulted from a desire to incorporate the latest developments: a flight deck angled at 6·5 degrees, steam catapults, 3-D radar and a deck edge lift. *Hermes* served as a conventional attack carrier until 1971, when she was taken in hand for conversion to a commando carrier, operating Wessex HU.5 helicopters in the vertical assault role. Four LCVPs were slung on davits beneath the after part of the flight deck, accommodation was expanded, and the catapults and arrestor gear were removed. *Hermes* served as a commando carrier from 1973 until 1976, when her role was again altered, this time to that of an antisubmarine carrier. Further modifications were made to equip her for this mission, but *Hermes* retains her LCVPs and can embark two commando groups (750 men) in the assault role.

An air group identical to that of the Invincible class is operated in peacetime. A 12-degree "ski-jump" ramp weighing 230 tons was constructed at the forward end of the flight deck during a refit 1980-81, and *Hermes* subsequently embarked her first Sea Harrier squadron. As flagship of the Falklands Task Force in 1982 *Hermes* embarked 12 Sea Harriers, 9 Sea King Mk 5 ASW helicopters, and 9 Sea King Mk 4 assault helicopters. At the height of operations in the South Atlantic she had no less than 21 fixed-wing aircraft embarked, including a number of RAF Harrier GR.3s.

Top right: *Hermes* on sea trials following the fitting of a 12-degree "ski jump" in May 1981. Three Sea Kings are lined up on the forward helo spots, and there are four Sea Harriers of 800 NAS aft. The fourth helicopter is a Wessex HU.5 (for SAR).

Right: *Hermes* returns to Portsmouth to a triumphant welcome in July 1982, her decks crowded with aircraft. At the height of the Falklands campaign she was operating no less than 21 Sea Harriers and Harrier GR.3s, in addition to Sea King ASW and transport helicopters. Wessex HU.5s can be seen aft.

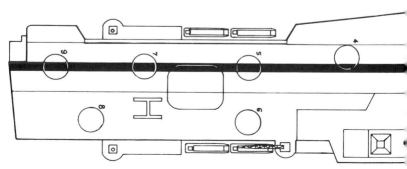

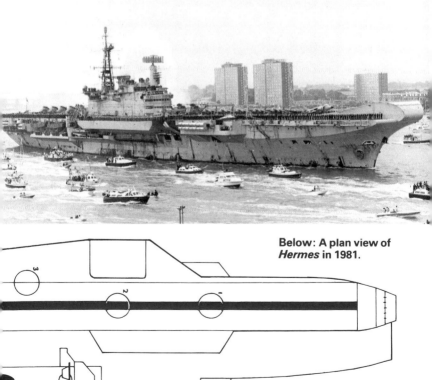

Below: A plan view of *Hermes* in 1981.

USSR
Kiev

Completed: 1975 onwards.
Names: *Kiev*; *Minsk*; *Novorossisk*; *Kharkov* (building).
Displacement: 33,000 tons standard; 38,000 tons full load.
Dimensions: Length overall 899ft (274m); beam 157ft 6in (48m); draught 33ft (10m).
Elevators: 1 inboard (fwd), 62ft x 33ft (19m x 10m); 1 inboard (aft), 62ft x 16ft 6in (19m x 5m).
Catapults: None.
Propulsion: 4-shaft geared steam turbines; 180,000shp = 32kt.
Armament: 8 SS-N-12 launchers (24 SSMs); 2 twin SA-N-3 launchers (72 Goblet SAMs); 2 twin SA-N-4 launchers (36 Gecko SAMs); 2 twin 76·2mm D-P guns; 8 30mm Gatling CIWS; twin SUW-N-1 launcher (20? ASW missiles); 2 RBU 6000 A/S rocket launchers; 2 quintuple banks of 21in (533mm) TT.
Aircraft: 12 Yak-36MP Forger; 18-21 Ka-25 Hormone A/B.
Complement: 1,700.

Developed from the Moskva class, the Tactical Aircraft-Carrying Cruisers of the Kiev class have a more conventional carrier flight deck arrangement to enable them to operate VTOL aircraft as well as helicopters. The forward part of the ship, however, remains that of a conventional cruiser, giving *Kiev* and her sisters a carrier/cruiser configuration without parallel in the West.

The primary mission of the Kiev class is ASW, and for this the ships carry an outfit of weapons systems almost identical to that of the Moskva class: a squadron of some 18 Ka-25 Hormone A helicopters, an SUW-N-1 launcher for FRAS-1 missiles, two rocket launchers and two quintuple banks of torpedo tubes. Target data is provided by a large low-frequency bow sonar and a variable depth sonar. The air defence systems, which are even more extensive than those of *Moskva*, are divided between the forecastle and the after end of the island superstructure, thereby giving complete all-round coverage. The island superstructure itself is exceptionally large because of the requirement to accommodate numerous surveillance and fire control radars. Four pairs of SS-N-12 launchers, located on the forecastle with a reload magazine between them, provide *Kiev* with a formidable anti-ship capability. (The SS-N-12 missiles replace, in effect, the air attack squadrons of the large-deck carriers of the US Navy). ▶

Above: The TAKR *Minsk* in the Far East. Ka-25 Hormone ASW helicopters can be seen on the after deck park. The starboard side of the ship is dominated by the massive island superstructure, which carries the air search and fire control radars associated with the ship's extensive weapons systems. Two boats are carried on davits in recesses on either side of the stern, and the accommodation ladder is amidships. Three Kievs are now in service; a fourth is completing.

Left: An artist's impression of *Minsk* undergoing maintenance in a large floating dock recently delivered to Vladivostok by Japanese shipyards. The dock measures 1,100ft (335m) by 290ft (80m) and has a capacity of 80,000 tons. A dock of similar size is also in service with the Northern Fleet.

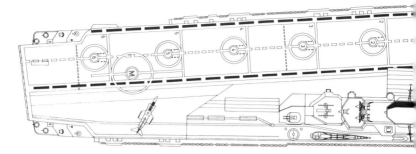

▶ The layout of the flight deck and aircraft-handling arrangements make it clear that *Kiev* was designed from the outset to operate the Yak-36 Forger VTOL aircraft. The flight deck is angled at 4 degrees, and in addition to its seven small helicopter spots has a large circle aft for Forger landings. The angled portion of the flight deck and the after deck park are covered with heat-resistant tiles to absorb the thrust of the Forger's two vertical-lift engines. The long, narrow hangar runs from beneath the forward end of the flight deck to the stern. The forward section of the hangar is probably about 49ft (15m) wide, and the broader after section about 69ft (21m). Between 30 and 35 aircraft could be accommodated, but there is no permanent deck park as in the big American carriers, probably because of the hostile weather conditions in which the Soviet vessels would operate from their bases in the Arctic and the Northwest Pacific. Hangar and flight deck are served by two aircraft lifts, one of which is twice the width of the other. The larger of the two

Above: An aerial view of *Kiev*. A Yak-36MP Forger VTOL strike fighter is ready for take-off on the flight deck aft, while six more Forgers are parked abreast the island superstructure, immediately forward of the larger of the two aircraft lifts. The second lift can just be made out at the after end of the island. The large cylindrical launchers visible on the forecastle are for SS-N-12 long-range anti-ship missiles; each launcher is provided with three weapons.

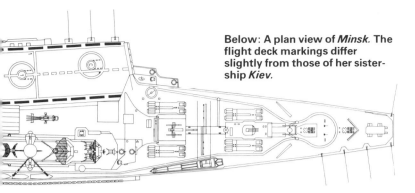

Below: A plan view of *Minsk*. The flight deck markings differ slightly from those of her sister-ship *Kiev*.

is amidships, between the angled deck and the island superstructure; the smaller is immediately aft of the island. There are several smaller elevators for deck tractors, personnel and munitions.

The Forger lacks the speed and endurance necessary for an effective interceptor, and the inability to make a rolling take-off (which in turn precludes a "ski-jump") imposes severe limitations on payload. It is probably more successful in the ground support role and may also be employed for reconnaissance, for driving away enemy surveillance and ASW patrol aircraft, and for attacks on small ships.

Kiev serves with the Soviet Northern Fleet and *Minsk* with the Pacific Fleet. *Novorossisk* has recently commissioned and will probably join the Northern Fleet, while *Kharkov* will not enter service until 1984. A large-deck carrier of a new type, probably with nuclear propulsion, is reported to be under construction in the Black Sea.

Above: An aerial view of *Kiev* on her first deployment to the Soviet Northern Fleet. There is a single Forger aft, and four Ka-25 Hormone ASW helicopters are lined up on the helo spots of the angled deck. The central door in the stern, which carries the ship's name in large letters, houses a towed variable depth sonar. 30mm Gatling mounts are disposed on either side of the stern for close-in defence; further Gatlings are carried before the bridge and on the port side forward.

USSR
Moskva

Completed: 1967-68.
Names: *Moskva*; *Leningrad*.
Displacement: 14,500 tons standard; 18,000 tons full load.
Dimensions: Length overall 625ft (190·5m); beam 112ft (34m); draught 25ft (7·6m).
Elevators: 2 inboard, 52ft x 15ft (16m x 4·6m).
Catapults: None.
Propulsion: 2-shaft geared steam turbines; 100,000shp = 30kt.
Armament: 2 twin SA-N-3 launchers (44 Goblet SAMs); 2 twin 57mm; twin SUW-N-1 launcher (20? ASW missiles); 2 RBU 6000 A/S rocket launchers.
Aircraft: 15-18 Ka-25 Hormone A.
Complement: 850.

Designed to hunt US Navy SSBNs operating in the Eastern Mediterranean, the Moskva class was almost certainly influenced by the helicopter cruisers built for the French and Italian navies during the early 1960s (see *Jeanne d'Arc* and

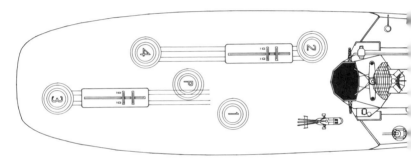

Vittorio Veneto). *Moskva* is, however, a much larger vessel, able to accommodate an air group of 15-18 Hormone A antisubmarine helicopters in a capacious hangar beneath her half-length flight deck. The latter is served by two aircraft lifts, and has a tractor garage at its forward end, set into the superstructure block with the flying control station above it. The narrowness of the lifts has proved a problem when helicopters other than the Hormone have been embarked; two Mi-8 Hip minesweeping helicopters operated by *Leningrad* in 1974 for the clearing of the Suez Canal had to remain on deck during the operation.

The forward half of the ship is occupied by a comprehensive suite of air defence systems. The SA-N-3 area defence and SUW-N-1 antisubmarine missile systems made their first appearance on this class and make the ships virtually self-escorting; a large hull-mounted low-frequency sonar and an independent variable depth sonar are fitted for sub-hunting operations. The massive block superstructure, which culminates in a tall pyramid-shaped uptake for the steam propulsion system, is built up in steps to accommodate the fire control and surveillance radars.

The Moskva class was limited to two units, and has been superseded by the Kiev class, which has its own embarked tactical VTOL fighters.

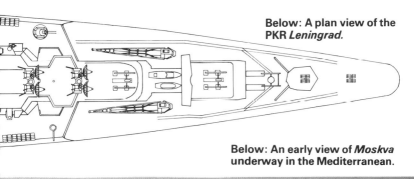

Below: A plan view of the PKR *Leningrad*.

Below: An early view of *Moskva* underway in the Mediterranean.

Nimitz

Completed: 1975 onwards.
Names: CVN 68 *Nimitz*; CVN 69 *Dwight D. Eisenhower*; CVN 70 *Carl Vinson*; CVN 71 *Theodore Roosevelt* (building).
Displacement: 81,600 tons standard; 91,400 tons full load.
Dimensions: Length overall 1,092ft (332·8m); beam 251ft (76·5m); draught 37ft (11·3m).
Elevators: 4 deck edge, 85ft x 52ft (25·9m x 15·9m), each 130,000lb (58,968kg) capacity.
Catapults: 4 steam C13-1.
Propulsion: 4-shaft nuclear; 2 A4W reactors; 260,000shp = 30kt.
Armament: 3 Sea Sparrow BPDMS launchers Mk 25 (1 x 8) in CVN 68-69; 3 NATO Sea Sparrow launchers Mk 29 (1 x 8) in CVN 70-71; 3 Phalanx CIWS in CVN 70-71.
Aircraft: 24 F-14A Tomcat; 24 A-7E Corsair; 10 A-6E Intruder + 4KA-6D; 4 E-2C Hawkeye; 4 EA-6B Prowler; 10 S-3A Viking; 6 SH-3H Sea King.
Complement: 3,073-3,151 + 2,625 (air wing).

The Nimitz class was originally envisaged as a replacement for the Midway class. The development of more advanced nuclear reactors made nuclear propulsion an increasingly attractive option, and the high initial cost associated with nuclear propulsion was accepted in return for the proven benefits of high endurance and reduced life-cycle costs. The two A4W reactors which power the Nimitz class each produce approximately 130,000shp compared with only 35,000shp for each of the eight A2W reactors installed in *Enterprise*. Moreover, the uranium cores need replacing less frequently than those originally used in *Enterprise*, giving a full 13-year period between refuellings. The reduction in the number of reactors from eight to two also allowed for major improvements in the internal arrangements below hangar deck level. Whereas in *Enterprise* the entire centre section of the ship is occupied by machinery rooms, with the aviation fuel compartments and the missile magazines pushed out towards the end of the ship, in *Nimitz* the propulsion machinery is divided into two separate units, with the magazines between them and forward of them. The improved layout has resulted in an increase of 20 per cent in aviation fuel capacity and a similar increase in the volume available for munitions and stores.

Flight deck layout is almost identical to that of *John F. Kennedy*. At hangar deck level, however, there has been a significant increase in the provision of maintenance workshops and spare parts stowage. Maintenance shops have ▶

Below: A plan view of *Nimitz* (CVN 68) with aircraft on deck.

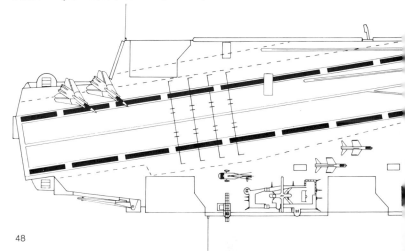

Below: Six F-14A Tomcats of VF-84 overfly *Nimitz* (CVN 68) at the end of her 144-day deployment to the Indian Ocean in 1980.

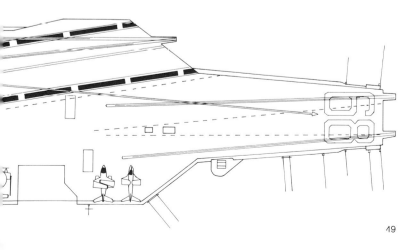

Above: *Dwight D. Eisenhower* (CVN 69) underway during an exercise in the Persian Gulf in January 1979. The most modern US carriers operate the F-14A Tomcat for Fleet Air Defence.

all but taken over the large sponson which supports the flight deck, and at the after end of the hangar there is a large bay for aero-engine maintenance and testing. The increased competition for internal volume even in a ship of this size is illustrated by the need to accommodate some 6,300 men (including air group) — the original Forrestal design on which *Nimitz* and her sisters are based provided for 3,800!

Sensor provision and defensive weapons are on a par with *John F. Kennedy*, although the third ship, *Carl Vinson,* has NATO Sea Sparrow and Phalanx in place of the BPDMS launchers of the earlier ships, which will be similarly fitted in the near future. *Vinson* is also fitted with an ASW control centre and specialised maintenance facilities for the S-3 Viking; these will also be installed in *Nimitz* and *Eisenhower* at future refits.

Delays in construction caused by shipyard problems resulted in rocketing costs, and in the late 1970s the Carter administration attempted, unsuccessfully, to block authorisation of funds for the construction of a fourth carrier in favour of the smaller, conventionally-powered CVV design. The CVV was never popular with the US Navy, however, and the Reagan administration has now committed itself to the continuation of the CVN programme, and two ships beyond *Theodore Roosevelt* are currently projected. *Nimitz* and *Eisenhower* serve in the Atlantic, *Vinson* in the Pacific.

Below: This early view of *Nimitz* (CVN 68) shows her with F-4J
Phantoms, A-7E Corsairs and E-2C Hawkeye AEW aircraft parked
forward. The F-4s have now been replaced by F-14As.

53

USA
Enterprise

Completed: 1961.
Names: CVN 65 *Enterprise*.
Displacement: 75,700 tons standard; 89,600 tons full load.
Dimensions: Length overall 1,123ft (342·3m); beam 248ft (75·6m); draught 36ft (11m).
Elevators: 4 deck-edge, 85ft x 52ft (25·9m x 15·9m), each 130,000lb (58,968kg) capacity.
Catapults: 4 steam C13.
Propulsion: 4-shaft nuclear; 8 A2W reactors; 280,000shp = 30kt.
Armament: 3 NATO Sea Sparrow launchers Mk 29 (3 x 8); 3 Phalanx CIWS.
Aircraft: 24 F-14A Tomcat; 24 A-7E Corsair; 10 A-6E Intruder + 4 KA-6D; 4 E-2C Hawkeye; 4 EA-6B Prowler; 10 S-3A Viking; 6 SH-3H Sea King.
Complement: 3,157 + 2,628 (air wing).

Laid down shortly after the US Navy's first nuclear-powered surface ship, the cruiser *Long Beach*, *Enterprise* was completed in the remarkably short space of 3 years 9 months. In order to provide sufficient power for a top speed of 30kt no less than eight nuclear reactors had to be accommodated, and the entire centre section of the ship below hangar deck level is taken up by machinery. *Enterprise* cost nearly twice as much to build as her fossil-fuelled contemporaries of the Kitty Hawk class but a number of strong arguments were advanced in favour of nuclear power: the nuclear-powered carrier would have reduced life-cycle costs due to infrequent refuellings, and would be capable of lengthy transits and continuous operations in high-threat areas at a high sustained speed. Moreover, the elimination of ship's fuel bunkers in *Enterprise* allowed a 50 per cent increase in aviation fuel capacity, and consequently in the number of consecutive days of strike operations she could sustain.

Below: *Enterprise* **participating in FLEETEX 1983 in the N.W. Pacific. New radars were fitted in a recent refit. The two carriers astern are** *Midway* **(CV 41) and** *Coral Sea* **(CV 43).**

Above: An early view of *Enterprise* operating F-4 Phantoms, A-4 Skyhawks and RA-5 Vigilantes. The F-4s have now been replaced by F-14 Tomcats, and the A-4s by A-7 Corsairs.

In size and general layout *Enterprise* is similar to the Kitty Hawk class. The most significant difference as completed was in the configuration of the island, a "box" structure on which "billboard" planar radar arrays were mounted. In a major refit 1979-81 this was replaced by a more conventional structure with rotating radars. *Enterprise* was to have received two Mk 10 launchers for Terrier missiles, but these were never installed and she is now fitted with a combination of NATO Sea Sparrow launchers and Phalanx CIWS guns. Since the mid-1960s *Enterprise* has operated with the Pacific Fleet.

Kitty Hawk

Completed: 1961-68.
Names: CV 63 *Kitty Hawk*; CV 64 *Constellation*; CV 66 *America*; CV 67 *John F. Kennedy*.
Displacement: 60,100-61,000 tons standard; 80,800-82,000 tons full load.
Dimensions: Length overall 1,048-1,073ft (319·4-327m); beam 250-268ft (76·2-81·7m); draught 36ft (11m).
Elevators: 4 deck edge, 85ft x 52ft (25·9m x 15·9m), each 130,000lb (58,968kg) capacity.
Catapults: 4 steam C13 in CV 63-64; 3 steam C13 + 1 steam C13-1 in CV 66-67.
Propulsion: 4-shaft geared steam turbines, 280,000shp = 30kt.
Armament: 2 twin Mk 10 launchers (40 + 40) for Terrier missiles in CV 64; 2 NATO Sea Sparrow launchers Mk 29 (2 x 8) in CV 63; 3 NATO Sea Sparrow launchers Mk 29 (3 x 8) in CV 66-67; 3 Phalanx CIWS.
Aircraft: 24 F-14A Tomcat; 24 A-7E Corsair; 10 A-6E Intruder + 4 KA-6D; 4 E-2C Hawkeye; 4 EA-6B Prowler; 10 S-3A Viking; 6 SH-3H Sea King.
Complement: 2,879-2,990 + 2,500 (air wing).

Although there are significant differences between the first pair completed and the last two vessels, these four carriers are generally grouped together because of their common propulsion system and flight deck layout.

Kitty Hawk and *Constellation* were ordered as improved Forrestals, incorporating a number of important modifications. The flight deck showed a slight increase in area, and the layout of the lifts was revised to improve aircraft-handling arrangements. The single port-side lift, which on the Forrestals was located at the forward end of the flight deck — and was therefore unusable during the landing operations — was repositioned at the after end of the overhang, outside the line of the angled deck. The respective positions of the centre lift on the starboard side and the island structure were reversed, so that two lifts were available to serve the forward catapults. A further improved feature of the lifts was that they were no longer strictly rectangular, but had an additional angled section at their forward end which enabled longer aircraft to be accommodated. The new arrangement proved so successful that it was adopted by all subsequent US carriers.

America, the third ship of the class, was completed after a gap of four years and therefore incorporated a number of further modifications. She has a narrower smokestack and is fitted with an SQS-23 sonar — the only US carrier so equipped. ▶

Above: *Kitty Hawk* (CV 63) underway in the Pacific Ocean. Four E-2C airborne early warning aircraft are parked forward of the island, together with an A-7E Corsair.

Left: *John F. Kennedy* (CV 67) off Puerto Rico in 1980. Although the flight deck layout is essentially the same as that of the earlier ships of the class, she can be distinguished by her canted stack and by the angle of the forward edge of the flight deck. The air wing comprises three attack squadrons, two fighter squadrons, fixed- and rotary-wing ASW squadrons, and a detachment of E-2C Hawkeyes for airborne early warning. Twelve F-14As can be distinguished on the after part of the flight deck. They are stowed with wings swept, VG fulfilling the same function in this respect as wing folding.

The first three ships were all completed with two Mk 10 launchers for Terrier missiles. The need to accommodate SPG-55 missile guidance radars in addition to a growing number of air surveillance antennae led to the adoption of a separate lattice mast abaft the island in this and subsequent classes.

In 1963 it was decided that the new carrier due to be laid down in FY 1964 would be nuclear-powered, but Congress baulked at the cost, and the ship was finally laid down as a conventionally-powered carrier of a modified Kitty Hawk design. *John F. Kennedy* can be distinguished externally from her near-sisters by her canted stack — designed to keep the corrosive exhaust gases clear of the flight deck — and by the shape of the forward end of the angled deck. She also abandoned the Terrier missile system, which consumed valuable space and merely duplicated similar area defence systems aboard the

carrier escorts, in favour of the Basic Point Defense Missile System (BPDMS). The earlier three vessels are at present being similarly modified, the Terrier launchers being removed and replaced by a combination of NATO Sea Sparrow and Phalanx CIWS guns.

Kitty Hawk and *Constellation* have served since completion in the Pacific. *America* and *John F. Kennedy* serve in the Atlantic, with frequent deployments to the Mediterranean.

Below: A recent view of *Constellation* (CV 64), with SPS-48 planar antenna atop the lattice mast in place of the earlier SPS-30. She is the only vessel of her class still armed with the Terrier area defence missile, which is now being phased out in favour of NATO Sea Sparrow.

USA
Forrestal

Completed: 1952-55.
Names: CV 59 *Forrestal*; CV 60 *Saratoga*; CV 61 *Ranger*; CV 62
Independence.
Displacement: 60,000 tons standard; 78,000 tons full load.
Dimensions: Length overall 1,039-1,047ft (316·7-319·1m); beam 238ft
(72·5m); draught 37ft (11·3m).
Elevators: 4 deck edge, 63ft x 52ft (19·2m x 15·8m), each 80,000lb (36,288kg)
capacity.
Catapults: 2 steam C7 + 2 steam C11-1 in CV 59-60; 4 steam C7 in CV 61-62.
Propulsion: 4-shaft geared steam turbines; 260,000-280,000shp = 33kt.
Armament: 2 Sea Sparrow BPDMS launchers Mk 25 (2 x 8) in CV 59-60; 2
NATO Sea Sparrow launchers Mk 29 (2 x 8) in CV 61-62.
Aircraft: 24 F-4J/S Phantom; 24 A-7E Corsair; 10 A-6E Intruder + 4 KA-6D; 4
E-2C Hawkeye; 4 EA-6B Prowler; 10 S-3A Viking; 6 SH-3H Sea King.
Complement: 2,848-2,911 + 2,500 (air wing).

Below: *Forrestal* **(CV 59) with the major part of her air complement on
deck. Unlike Soviet and West European air-capable ships, whose
complement of aircraft is governed by hangar size, US Navy carriers
expect to operate with some 50 per cent of their aircraft exposed to the
elements.**

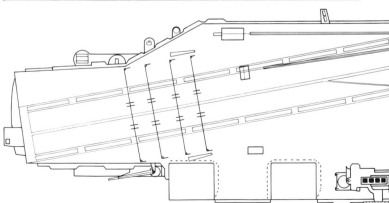

The overall size and the aircraft-handling arrangements of the Forrestal class were dictated by the requirement to operate the A-3 Skywarrior strategic bomber, which weighed fully 78,000lb (35,380kg). Hangar height was increased from 17ft 6in (5·3m) in the Midway class to 25ft (7·6m), and aviation fuel capacity from 365,000 gallons to 750,000 gallons. The original design was for a carrier similar in configuration to the ill-fated *United States*, which had a flush deck, together with a retractable bridge, and two waist catapults angled out on sponsons in addition to the customary pair of catapults forward. The advent of the angled deck, which was tested by the US Navy in 1952 on the Essex-class carrier *Antietam*, led to the modification of *Forrestal* while building to incorporate this new development. The result was the distinctive configuration which has been adopted by all subsequent US carrier construction: a massive flight deck with considerable overhang, and a small island incorporating the smokestack to starboard. Deck-edge lifts were incorporated in the overhang, resulting in a large uninterrupted hangar in which more than half the ship's aircraft could be accommodated. As completed the Forrestal class was armed with eight 5in (127mm) single gun mountings, but these were steadily removed and by the late 1970s had been replaced by BPDMS and NATO Sea Sparrow missile launchers.

Unlike later carriers the Forrestal class ships do not operate the F-14 Tomcat but retain the F-4 Phantom. *Ranger* serves in the Pacific, and the other three in the Atlantic. *Saratoga* was taken in hand in October 1980 for a three-year major modernisation (Service Life Extension Program, SLEP) which will enable her to remain operational into the 1990s. The other three ships will follow.

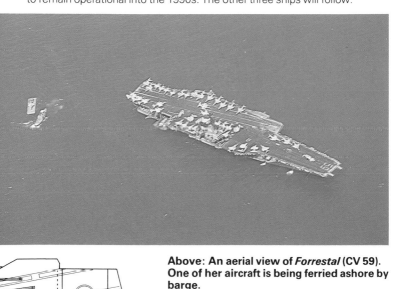

Above: An aerial view of *Forrestal* (CV 59). One of her aircraft is being ferried ashore by barge.

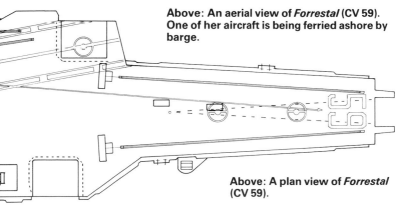

Above: A plan view of *Forrestal* (CV 59).

USA
Midway

Completed: 1945-47.
Names: CV 41 *Midway*; CV 43 *Coral Sea*.
Displacement: 51-52,000 tons standard; 64,000 tons full load.
Dimensions: Length overall 979ft (298·4m); beam 236-259ft (71·9-78·9m);
draught 36ft (11m).
Elevators: 3 deck edge, 63ft x 52ft (19·2m x 15·8m), 130,000lb (58,968kg)
capacity in CV 41; 3 deck edge, 56ft x 44ft (17m x 13·4m), 74,000lb (33,566kg)
capacity in CV 43.
Catapults: 2 steam C13 in CV 41; 3 steam C11-1 in CV 43.
Propulsion: 4-shaft geared steam turbines; 212,000shp = 32kt.
Armament: 2 Sea Sparrow BPDMS launchers Mk 25 (2 x 8) in CV 41; 3
Phalanx CIWS in both.
Aircraft: 24 F-4J/S Phantom; 24 A-7E Corsair; 10 A-6E Intruder + 4 KA-6D; 4
E-2C Hawkeye; 4 EA-6B Prowler.
Complement: 2,523-2,616 + 1,945 (air wing).

These ships were the last war-built US carriers. Three units were completed,
but *Franklin D. Roosevelt* was stricken in 1977. As built, the Midway class had
an axial flight deck with two centre-line lifts and a deck-edge lift amidships on
the port side. The original design was quickly overtaken by developments in jet

aircraft and the class underwent a major modernisation during the 1950s in which an 8-degree angled deck was constructed, the after lift moved to the deck edge position, C-11 catapults installed, and the armament reduced. *Coral Sea*, the last of the three to be modernised, incorporated a number of further modifications as a result of experience with her two sisters and with the Forrestal class. The port-side deck-edge lift was moved farther aft to clear the angled deck, and the forward centre-line lift replaced by a new deck-edge lift forward of the island. This conversion was particularly successful and *Coral Sea* remained largely unaltered throughout the 1960s and 1970s.

In 1966 *Midway* underwent a second major modernisation to enable her to operate the same aircraft as the more modern US carriers. The flight deck was completely rebuilt — its total area was increased by one third — and new lifts of greater capacity but similar in layout to those of *Coral Sea* installed. Two C-13 catapults were installed forward. BPDMS missile launchers replaced what remained of the original armament in 1979.

Midway is due to remain in service until 1988. *Coral Sea* has been reactivated to replace *Saratoga*, which is currently undergoing a Service Life Extension Program (SLEP), but she will subsequently become a training ship. Both ships are currently serving with the Pacific Fleet, and both operate as attack carriers, without fixed- or rotary-wing ASW aircraft.

Below: *Coral Sea* (CV 43), reactivated to replace *Saratoga,* returns from deployment to the Western Pacific in 1982.

USA
Tarawa

Completed: 1976-80.
Names: LHA 1 *Tarawa*; LHA 2 *Saipan*; LHA 3 *Belleau Wood*; LHA 4 *Nassau*;
LHA 5 *Peleliu*.
Displacement: 39,300 tons full load.
Dimensions: Length overall 820ft (249·9m); beam 126ft (38·4m); draught
26ft (7·9m).
Elevators: 1 stern-line, 59ft 9in x 34ft 9in (18·2m x 10·6m), 80,000lb
(36,288kg) capacity; 1 deck edge, 50ft x 34ft (15·2m x 10·4m), 40,000lb
(18,144kg) capacity.
Catapults: None.
Propulsion: 2-shaft geared steam turbines; 70,000shp = 24kt.
Armament: 2 BPDMS launchers Mk 25 (2 x 8); 3 single 5in (127mm) Mk 45.
Aircraft: 30 helicopters/VTOL aircraft (AV-8A, CH-53D, CH-46D, AH-1T, UH-
1N, see text).
Complement: 900 (+ 2,000 troops).

Below: A plan view of *Tarawa* (LHA -1).

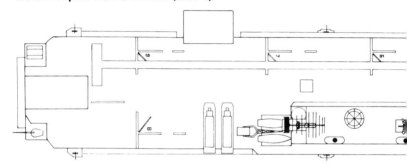

The Tarawa-class LHAs are large amphibious vessels combining in a single hull capabilities which previously had required a number of separate specialist types. They incorporate both an aircraft hangar and a docking-well for landing craft, and can therefore employ "vertical" or "horizontal" assault techniques. The hangar is located in the after part of the ship directly above the docking-well; both are 268ft in length and 78ft wide (81·7m x 23·8m), and the hangar has a 20ft (6·1m) overhead to enable the latest heavy-lift helicopters to be accommodated. A typical loading of helicopters would include 9-12 CH-46 Sea Knights, six CH-53D Sea Stallions, four AH-1 SeaCobra gunships and 2-4 UH-1 utility helicopters. Detachments of AV-8A Harriers are frequently embarked, and in a recent NATO exercise no less than 11 such aircraft operated from the deck of *Nassau*.

The docking-well can accommodate four LCUs, and is served by an elaborate cargo transfer system employing a central conveyor belt and 11 overhead monorail cars. Forward of the docking-well is a "multi-storey car park" for tanks, guns, trucks and LVTP-7 amphibious personnel carriers. Above the vehicle decks there is accommodation for both the Commander Amphibious Task Group (CATG) and the Landing Force Commander (LFC) and their respective staffs. These ships generally serve as flagships of Marine amphibious squadrons. The essentially defensive armament includes three lightweight 5in (127mm) guns for fire support operations.

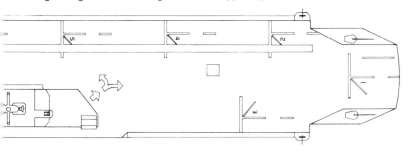

Left: An aerial view of *Tarawa*. Note the vertical sides, necessary to accommodate the large docking well aft, with the helicopter hangar above. The two 5-inch guns forward are for fire support as well as for air defence, and one of the two BPDMS launchers can be seen forward of the large island superstructure. Nine helo spots are available for the ship's assault helicopters, and the broad continuous line to port is used for rolling take-offs by the AV-8A Harrier V/STOL aircraft, of which a detachment of four is generally carried. The lifts serving the flight deck are both located aft, and two LCM-6 landing craft are carried abaft the island. The Tarawa class was originally to have comprised nine ships, but financial constraints reduced it to one of five.

USA
Iwo Jima

Completed: 1961-70.
Names: LPH 2 *Iwo Jima*; LPH 3 *Okinawa*; LPH 7 *Guadalcanal*; LPH 9 *Guam*;
LPH 10 *Tripoli*; LPH 11 *New Orleans*; LPH 12 *Inchon*.
Displacement: 17,000 tons light: 18,300 tons full load.
Dimensions: Length overall 592ft (180·4m); beam 112ft (34·1m); draught
26ft (7·9m).
Elevators: 2 deck edge, 50ft x 34ft (15·2m x 10·4m); 50,000lb (22,680kg)
capacity in LPH 2-3, 11-12; 44,000lb (19,958kg) capacity in LPH 7, 9-10.
Catapults: None.
Propulsion: 1-shaft geared steam turbines; 22,000shp = 20kt.
Armament: 2 BPDMS launchers Mk 25 (2 x 8); 2 twin 3in (76mm) Mk 33.
Aircraft: 25 helicopters (CH-46D, CH-53D, AH-1T, UH-1N).
Complement: 652 (+ 2000 troops).

The US Marine Corps had initiated experiments in helicopter assault
techniques as early as 1948, and following the conversion of the former escort
carrier *Thetis Bay* in 1955 to test the "vertical envelopment" concept the
construction of a series of specialised assault ships (LPH) was begun. As the
ships of the *Iwo Jima* class were amphibious — not fleet — units, an austere
design based on a mercantile hull with a single-shaft propulsion system was
adopted. The large central hangar has 20ft (6·1m) clearance, a capacity of
about 20 helicopters, and has deck-edge lifts disposed en echelon at either
end. The latter fold upwards to close the hangar openings when not in use.
Fore and aft of the hangar there is accommodation for a Marine battalion of
some 2,000 men, and there is a well-equipped hospital with 300 beds. The
flight deck is marked out with five helo spots along the port side and two to
starboard. Helicopter assault operations are directed from a specialised
Command Centre housed in the island. The radar outfit is austere, and the
armament, which now includes two BPDMS launchers, is for self-defence
only.

From 1972 until 1974 *Guam* was test ship for the Sea Control Ship concept
(see also *Príncipe de Asturias*). In this role she operated ASW helicopters and a
squadron of Marine AV-8A Harriers. A new tactical command centre was
installed and carrier-controlled approach radar fitted. Although operations with
the Harrier were particularly successful the Sea Control Ship did not find favour
with the US Navy, and *Guam* has since reverted to the assault ship role.

Although *Inchon*, the last ship built, carries two LCVPs, the LPHs have no
significant ability to land troops, equipment and supplies by any means other
than by helicopter. They generally operate in conjunction with ships of the
LPD, LSD and LST types.

**Below: A plan view of an assault ship of the Iwo Jima class. Note the
deck-edge lifts offset to port and to starboard.**

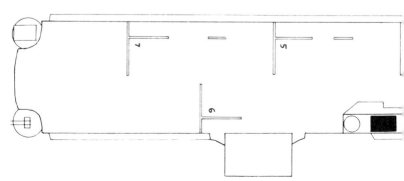

Above: *Guam* (LPH 9) underway, with Marine assault helicopters amidships. Note the large helo circles in this early view.

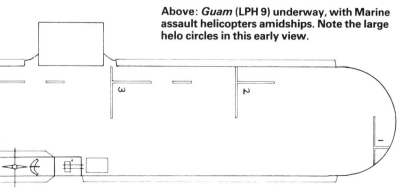

Shipborne Aviation

Aérospatiale Alouette III

Type: (SA 316, SA 319) shipborne multi-role helicopter (crew of 1).
Data: SA 319 (Alouette III).
Dimensions: Length of fuselage 32ft 10¾in (10·03m); main rotor diameter 36ft 1¾in (11·02m); height 9ft 10in (3m).
Weight: Empty 2,520lb (1,143kg); maximum 4,850lb (2,200kg).
Engines: One 600shp Turbomeca Artouste XIV turboshaft.
Performance: Maximum speed 113kt (210km/h); service ceiling 10,500ft (3,200m); range 259nm (480km).
Payload: 1/2 Mk 44 homing torpedoes or 2 AS.12 ASMs.
History: First flight (SA 316) Feb 1959; (SA 319B) 1967.
Users: France (Aéronavale); Argentina, Belgium, Chile, Denmark, Ecuador, Greece, India, Indonesia, S. Korea, Libya, Mexico, Pakistan, Peru, Sweden.

The Aérospatiale Alouette is a light multi-purpose helicopter which is operated in a variety of roles by many of the world's air forces and navies. Most navies operate the Alouette in the liaison/utility role, but until the advent of the Lynx the Astazou-powered SA 319B Alouette III was the standard light shipborne helicopter in service with the French Navy. It served aboard frigates and destroyers in the ASW role, armed with one or two Mk 44 homing torpedoes, and in the surface attack role, armed with AS.12 missiles. Alouette IIIs are still used for plane guard duties on the French carriers.

Aérospatiale Dauphin 2

Type: (SA 365F) shipborne surface attack helicopter (crew of 2); (SA 365F, HH-65A Dolphin) shipborne patrol and SAR helicopter.
Data: SA 365F.
Dimensions: Fuselage length 39ft 8¾in (12·11m); main rotor diameter 39ft 1¾in (11·93m); height 13ft 1in (3·99m).
Weight: Empty 4,720lb (2,141kg); maximum 8,598lb (3,900kg).
Engines: Two 710shp Turboméca Arriel 1C free-turbine turboshafts.
Performance: Maximum speed 170kt (315km/h); service ceiling 15,000ft (4,575m); range 300nm (555km).
Payload: 4 AS.15TT ASMs.
History: First flight (SA 360) June 1972; (SA 365) Jan 1975.
Users: Saudi Arabia, US Coast Guard.

The Dauphin was designed by Aérospatiale as a successor to the Alouette. It incorporates advanced features such as the Fenestron tail rotor, anti-vibration systems and composite blades. It is in production for the US Coast Guard as the HH-65A. Twenty SA 365 surface attack and four SA 365 SAR variants are on order for Saudi Arabia. The SA 365Fs will operate from the new missile frigates under construction in France, and will carry up to four AS.15 anti-ship missiles. They will be fitted with a Thomson-CSF Agrion pulse-doppler radar (derived from the Iguane developed as a retrofit to the Breguet Alize aircraft) to permit mid-course guidance of Otomat SSMs carried by the ships. An alternative antisubmarine variant, the SA 365AS, has been proposed, with search radar and dipping sonar, or Agrion 15, MAD and homing torpedoes.

The aircraft in this section can all be operated from surface ships. Many were designed for operation from carriers or from smaller surface vessels such as ASW frigates; others have been adapted from land-based models for shipboard use in a variety of roles.

Above: An Alouette III with AS.12 anti-ship missiles. The Alouette is now used mainly as a liaison helicopter.

Above: An SA 365F Dauphin 2 with four AS.15TT anti-ship missiles and the Agrion 15 fire control radar.

Aérospatiale Super Frelon

Type: (SA 321G, SA 321M) shipborne/land based antisubmarine helicopter (crew of 5); (SA 321Ja) transport helicopter (crew of 2).
Data: SA 321G.
Dimensions: Fuselage length 63ft 7¾in (19·4m); main rotor diameter 62ft (18·9m); height 16ft 2½in (4·9m).
Weight: Empty 15,130lb (6,863kg); maximum 28,660lb (13,000kg).
Engines: Three 1,570shp Turboméca Turmo IIIC$_6$ turboshafts.
Performance: Maximum speed 148kt (275km/h); service ceiling 10,325ft (3,150m); range 440nm (815km); mission endurance 4hr.
Payload: (SA 321G) 4 Mk 44/46 homing torpedoes or 2 AM.39 ASMs; (SA 321 Ja) 27-31 troops or 11,025lb (5,000kg) cargo.
History: First flight (SA 3210) Dec 1962; (SA 321G) Nov 1965; service delivery 1966.
Users: France (Aéronavale); China (on order), Iraq, Libya.

The Super Frelon is the largest helicopter to be designed and built in Western Europe. It is derived from Aérospatiale's own SA 3200 Frelon but incorporates technology borrowed from other companies. The main lift and tail rotors and their drive systems were designed with assistance from Sikorsky, and Fiat assisted with the main gearbox and power transmission. The Super Frelon is built in two main variants: the SA 321G all-weather antisubmarine model, and the SA 321 Ja transport version. Twenty-four Super Frelon SA 321 Gs were built for the Aéronavale, ten serve with 32F in the ASW role, and the remainder as transport helicopters with 27F and 33F. A number of Super Frelon SA 321 Gs of 32F have operated from one or other of the carriers of the Clemenceau class in recent years, and 32F is also responsible for antisubmarine operations in support of France's ballistic-missile submarines. The SA 321 Gs generally operate in groups of up to four helicopters, with one employing its Sylphe panoramic dunking sonar for listening while the others make their attacks. They are currently being refurbished, and will be equipped with the ORB32 Héraclès II search radar, which doubles the detection range of the Héraclès I and is compatible with the AM.39 Exocet anti-ship missile.

The Libyan Air Force operates nine SA 321 Ms in the ASW/SAR roles. Iraq operates ten Super Frelon armed with AM.39 Exocet ASMs for surface attack, and has a further three on order. The People's Republic of China has purchased 13 Super Frelons for its navy for use as transport helicopters.

Above: A Super Frelon of the
Aéronavale deploys its dunking
sonar. Ten ASW models serve
with 32F.

Below: A Super Frelon of 32F
conducts trials with the AM.39
missile. Iraq operates Super
Frelons in the anti-ship role.

Below: An SA 321G Super Frelon of the Aéronavale. This particular
model is for search and rescue (SAR). It lacks the ORB 32 Héraclès I radar
fitted to antisubmarine models. The Super Frelon is the largest
helicopter to be designed and built in Western Europe; the rotors and
drive systems are based on American technology, whilst the main
gearbox and transmission were designed by the Italian Fiat company.

Breguet Alizé

Type: (Br.1050) three-seat carrier-based antisubmarine aircraft.
Dimensions: Length 45ft 6in (13·9m); span 51ft 2in (15·6m); height 15ft 7in (4·75m).
Weight: Empty 12,570lb (5,700kg); maximum 18,190lb (8,250kg).
Engines: One 1,975shp Rolls-Royce Dart RDa. 21 single-shaft turboprop.
Performance: Maximum speed 248kt (460km/h) at sea level; service ceiling 20,500ft (6,250m); range 1,350nm (2,500km); mission endurance 4hr 30min.
Payload: Weapons bay for homing torpedo or depth charges; underwing racks for 2 AS.12 missiles, rockets, bombs or depth charges.
History: First flight (Br. 1050 prototype) Oct 1956; service delivery March 1959.
Users: France (Aéronavale); India.

Below: Alizé antisubmarine aircraft of the Marine Nationale comes in to land. The retractable radome which houses the search radar can be See number forward of the tail-hook. The Wing Nacelles carry sonobuoys and there are weapons pylons between them and racks on the outside.

Below: An Alizé of the Indian Navy. Those remaining in service are currently undergoing a major overhaul of their electronics.

In 1948 initial design work began in France on a home-grown carrier-based strike aircraft, which became the Vultur (Br. 960). An unusual configuration was adopted, with a Rolls-Royce Nene jet at the back and a turboprop in the nose — an arrangement designed to provide a good combat radius (using only the turboprop) combined with high performance in the strike area. The Vultur was not proceeded with, and in 1954 it was decided to convert it into an antisubmarine aircraft. The turbojet was replaced by a retractable radome, and sonobuoys were located in two wing nacelles. An internal weapons bay can accommodate a homing torpedo or depth bombs, and there are also two underwing pylons for additional ordnance. The pilot and a radar operator sit side by side beneath a broad cockpit canopy, and there is a second systems operator in a side-facing seat behind them.

Seventy-five Alizés were built for the carriers *Clemenceau* and *Foch*, and 20 of these remain in service with 4F and 6F. Twelve Alizés were also delivered to India for service aboard the carrier *Vikrant*. The Alizé has proved successful and reliable in service, but no replacement is envisaged by the French. Twenty-eight aircraft have now been modernised to keep them in service until the end of the decade. An Iguane sea radar and a new acoustics processor have been fitted. The Alizés remain in service with Indian Navy are also to be updated while the carrier *Vikrant* undergoes modernisation, and will probably remain in service for some years yet.

Above: The Alizé has been in service for more than 20 years with the Marine Nationale and, following a recent refurbishment, is expected to continue in service until the end of the decade.

INDIAN NAVY

Dassault-Breguet Super Etendard

Type: Single-seat carrier-based strike fighter.
Dimensions: Length 46ft 11½in (14·3m); span 31ft 5¾in (9·6m); height 12ft 8in (3·85m).
Weight: Empty 14,220lb (6,450kg); maximum 25,350lb (11,500kg).
Engines: One 11,265lb (5,110kg) thrust SNECMA Atar 8K-50 single-shaft turbojet.
Performance: Maximum speed 637kt (1,180km/h) at sea level; service ceiling 45,000ft (13,700m); range 1,080nm (2,000km); combat radius 350nm (650km).
Payload: 2 30mm DEFA cannon; 1 centre-line and 4 wing pylons for total load of 4,630lb (2,100kg).
History: First flight (converted Etendard) Oct 1974; first delivery 1978.
Users: France (Aéronavale); Argentina.

The original Etendard IV was developed as a light "strike fighter" to operate from the carriers *Foch* and *Clemenceau*. Sixty-nine of the IVM attack version and 21 of the IVP photo-reconnaissance variant were built, and two mixed squadrons of Etendard aircraft, each comprising eight IVM plus two IVP,

Below: A Super Etendard is lined up for take-off on the forward catapult of the French carrier *Clemenceau*. The Super Etendard will replace not only the Etendard IVM but, eventually, also the F-8E Crusader. The major shortcoming of the aircraft is its limited range. Argentine Navy aircraft operating from land bases during the Falklands conflict were armed with an AM.39 missile beneath one wing and carried a drop tank beneath the other.

served on both French carriers until the late 1970s. It was first envisaged that the Etendard would be replaced by a navalised Jaguar, but following the cancellation of this project on political and cost grounds it was decided to opt for an improved Etendard, which became the Super Etendard. Flight development using three converted Etendard IVs took place 1974-77, and the Super Etendard began replacing the IVM (but not the IVP, which remains in service with 16F) in first-line squadrons in 1979. The airframe of the Super Etendard has been substantially redesigned for higher airspeeds and weights, and a new, more efficient engine and inertial navigation system were produced in France with US help. A new multi-mode radar developed by Thomson CSF in collaboration with Electronique Marcel Dassault gives especially good performance in the low-level surface attack role, for which the Super Etendard is fitted with the AM.39 Exocet missile. The aircraft also has a nuclear strike capability

Initially 100 aircraft were to have been purchased for the Aéronavale, but the order was subsequently cut to 71, 36 of which now serve in three *flotilles* — 11F, 14F, and 17F. In 1979 Argentina ordered 14 Super Etendards to replace the A-4Q Skyhawks aboard its carrier *25 de Mayo* and although only five had been delivered by April 1982, these quickly made their mark on the Falklands conflict, sinking both the destroyer *Sheffield* and the container ship *Atlantic Conveyor* with Exocet missiles. A reconnaissance version is under consideration for the Aéronavale to replace the Etendard IVP. Purchases are also sought by several countries, including Iraq and Libya, so an extended production run seems likely.

Agusta-Bell 204

Type: (AB 204AS) shipborne antisubmarine helicopter (crew of 3).
Dimensions: Fuselage length 40ft 4¾in (12·3m); main rotor diameter 48ft (14·6m); height 14ft 4¾in (4·4m).
Weight: Empty 4,600lb (2,090kg); maximum 9,501lb (4,310kg).
Engines: One 1,290shp General Electric T58-3 or RR Gnome turboshaft.
Performance: Maximum speed 104kt (193km/h); service ceiling 10,500ft (3,200m); range 216nm (400km); operational radius 60nm (110km).
Payload: 2 Mk 44/46 homing torpedoes or 4 AS.12 ASMs.
History: First flight 1961; service delivery 1964.
Users: Italy.

The AB 204 was developed from the Bell Iroquois and serves as a utility helicopter in the Regia Aeronautica and the armed forces of a number of other countries. The ASW variant, the AB 204AS, was built for operation from a series of antisubmarine cruisers and frigates built for the Italian Navy during the 1960s. The helicopters work in pairs, one being fitted with an AQS-13B dunking sonar and the other with two MK 44/46 homing torpedoes. Some two dozen AB 204s remain in service, but they are being steadily replaced by the newer AB 212.

Agusta-Bell 212

Type: (AB 212ASW) shipborne antisubmarine helicopter (crew of 3-4).
Dimensions: Fuselage length 45ft 11¼in (14m); main rotor diameter 48ft (14·6m); height 12ft 10¼in (3·9m).
Weight: Empty 7,540lb (3,420kg); maximum 11,200lb (5,080kg).
Engines: One 1,875shp United Aircraft of Canada PT6T-3 Turbo Twin Pac.
Performance: Maximum speed 106kt (196km/h); service ceiling 14,200ft (4,330m); range 315nm (584km); mission endurance 3hr.
Payload: 2 Mk 44/46 homing torpedoes or 4 AS.12 ASMs.
History: First flight (Bell 212) 1969; service delivery (AB 212) 1978.
Users: Italy; Ecuador, Greece, Iran, Iraq, Peru, Turkey, Venezuela.

Although similar in overall dimensions to the AB 204 which it is replacing aboard Italian surface ships, the AB 212 represents a great advance in capabilities over its predecessor. A more powerful search radar is fitted in a radome above the cabin, and sonobuoys are carried in addition to the AQS-13B dunking sonar. Four AS.12 missiles can be carried in the surface attack role, and the TG-2 system enables the AB 212 to provide mid-course guidance to ship-launched Otomat SSMs. Forty-eight AB 212s are on order for the Italian Navy, and ASW variants have also been purchased by Greece, Iraq, Peru, Turkey and Venezuela. Peru and Venezuela will operate the AB 212 from Italian-built frigates of the Lupo class, while Greece will operate the helicopter from two "Standaard"-class frigates purchased from the Netherlands. The AB 212 extends still further the basic Huey/Iroquois design, which was originally drawn up nearly 30 years ago.

Right: An AB 212 antisubmarine helicopter of the Italian Navy deploying its AQS-13B dunking sonar. The AB 212 is extraordinarily well-equipped for its size. Besides ASW operations, for which it carries two Mk 46 homing torpedoes, it can perform in the surface strike role. It can also provide mid-course guidance for Otomat anti-ship missiles launched by the latest destroyers and frigates of the Italian Navy. The prominent "pot" above the cabin is for a surface search radar. The Italian Navy has persisted with the skid undercarriage in the face of a preference for castored wheels on the part of other navies.

Above: An AB 204B is seen here aboard the Bergamini class frigate *Carlo Margottini*. Although primarily used for ASW, Italian shipborne helicopters also have a ship-strike role which is essential to the independent surface operations favoured by the Italian Navy. AB 204s are currently being superseded by more capable AB 212s.

BAe Sea Harrier

Type: (FRS.1) single-seat carrier-based strike fighter.
Dimensions: Length 47ft 7in (14·5m); span 25ft 3in (7·7m); height 12ft 2in (3·7m).
Weight: Empty 12,500lb (5,670kg); maximum 22,500lb (10,206kg).
Engines: One 21,500lb (9,752kg) thrust Roll-Royce Pegasus 104 vectored-thrust turbofan.
Performance: Maximum speed 640kt (1,185km/h) at sea level; service ceiling 50,000ft (15,240m); ferry range 1,800mm (3,330km); combat radius (fighter) 400nm (750km) with allowance for combat and VL, (strike) 280nm (520km).
Payload: 2 30mm Aden cannon; (fighter) 2-4 AIM-9 Sidewinder AAMs plus 2 drop tanks; (strike) 1 centre-line and 4 wing stations for bombs or ASMs; maximum total load 8,000lb (3,628kg).
History: First flight (FRS.1) Aug 1978; service delivery June 1979.
Users: UK (RN); India.

▶

Below: Two Sea Harriers of 800 Naval Air Squadron land aboard HMS _Hermes_. Both are armed with an AIM-9L Sidewinder AAM on the port outer pylon, and carry drop tanks on the inner pylons. Larger 190-gallon drop tanks were introduced during the Falklands conflict to increase time on patrol, and a more recent modification has been a "doubling-up" of the outer weapons stations to enable two pairs of Sidewinders to be carried. Note the twin Aden cannon pods in the belly.

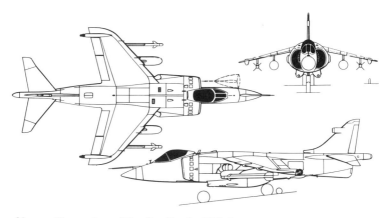

Above: Three-view of the Sea Harrier FRS.1.

In the early 1960s a new VTOL aircraft developed from the P.1127 Kestrel, the P.1154, was proposed for joint service with the Royal Navy and the Royal Air Force. The Navy requirement, however, was for a two-seat interceptor while the RAF wanted a single-seat ground attack aircraft, and it proved impossible to accommodate these conflicting requirements within the same airframe. It was decided in 1964 that the Navy's new carrier, CVA-01, would operate only conventional fixed-wing aircraft, but in 1966 both the CVA-01 and the P.1154 were cancelled. The RAF was left to develop the Kestrel for the close support role, but the Navy was compelled to rethink its requirements. With the phasing out of large-deck carriers during the 1970s, the Through-Deck Cruiser (TDC) would be the only air-capable ship on the drawing board, and she was designed to operate only ASW helicopters from a flight deck of modest dimensions, without catapults or arrestor wires. The only possibility of ensuring a continuation of fixed-wing operations in the Royal Navy therefore lay in V/STOL aircraft. Even so, the decision to order the Sea Harrier was taken only in 1975, when *Invincible* had already been under construction for three years.

The Sea Harrier is basically an RAF GR.3 with a marinised Pegasus Mk 103 engine (designated Mk 104) and a completely redesigned forward fuselage. The cockpit was raised 11in (280mm) to provide increased space for mission avionics, and a fuller canopy was adopted to further improve rearward visibility. The nose was enlarged to accommodate a Ferranti Blue Fox multi-mode radar developed from the Sea Spray radar of the HAS.2 Lynx. Blue Fox can operate in the airborne search and intercept, and the air-to-surface search and strike modes. The changes from the basic Harrier design — the airframe and engine have 90 per cent commonality with the GR.3 but the weapon systems and avionics are 90 per cent new — reflect in part the need for the

Sea Harrier to operate in a maritime environment, but also a significant change of role from close support to fleet air defence and maritime strike (hence the FRS — Fighter Reconnaissance Strike — designation). Aluminium alloys were substituted for magnesium components in order to combat salt corrosion, an emergency braking system installed, and tie-down lugs provided on the undercarriage. The weapon hardpoints were strengthened with new ejection release units, and a missile control panel was installed in the cockpit for handling AIM-9 Sidewinder AAMs (outer wing pylons) and Harpoon/Sea Eagle ASMs (inner pylons). The development of the "ski jump" ramp has provided considerable payload benefits when a short rolling take-off is employed.

Initial Royal Navy orders were for 34 aircraft, and no less than 28 of these saw service in the South Atlantic during the Falklands conflict. Besides the first-line squadrons operational with *Hermes* (800) and *Invincible* (801), 809 and 899 (HQ) squadrons provided additional aircraft to boost the carrier air groups. The Sea Harrier was used extensively in the fleet air defence role, armed with Sidewinder AAMs on the outer pylons and with drop tanks on the inner pylons to improve combat radius, and was also employed in the land attack role. Six aircraft were lost (two to ground fire and the others in flying accidents), and these are to be replaced by new construction, an additional seven aircraft being ordered at the same time to make up the third carrier air squadron. The only other nation so far to purchase the Sea Harrier is India, which has ordered six FRS.51s plus two T.60 trainers to replace its elderly Sea Hawks on the carrier *Vikrant*.

Below: Sea Harriers of 800 (near camera), 801 and 809 NAS in the overall dark sea grey paint scheme introduced as a result of the Falklands operation.

Westland/Aérospatiale Lynx

Type: (HAS.2, HAS.3) shipborne antisubmarine/strike helicopter (crew of two).

Dimensions: Fuselage length 39ft 7in (12·1m); main rotor diameter 42ft (12·8m); height 11ft 6in (3·5m).

Weight: Empty (basic) 6,680lb (3,030kg), (with dunking sonar) 7,370lb (3,343kg); maximum 10,500lb (4,763kg).

Engines: Two 900shp Rolls-Royce Gem 10001, or 1,120shp Gem 41-1 three-shaft turbines.

Performance: Maximum speed 145kt (269km/h); service ceiling 12,000ft (3,658m); range 320nm (593km); mission endurance (max) 2hr 50 min.

Payload: (ASW) 2 Mk 46 or Stingray homing torpedoes or 2 Mk 11 depth bombs; (surface strike) 4 AS.12 or Sea Skua ASMs.

History: First flight March 1971; service delivery May 1976.

Users: UK (RN), France (Aéronavale); Argentina, Brazil, Denmark, FRG, Netherlands, Nigeria, Norway.

Developed by Westland as a multi-role helicopter, the WG.13 Lynx is built in 70/30 partnership with Aérospatiale of France. The avionics are tailored to one-man operation in all-weather, and the Lynx has distinguished itself by its agility and versatility. The naval variants have a castored tricycle landing gear for improved deck-handling and a folding tail section. The standard version ordered for the Royal Navy is the HAS.2, which is fitted with a Sea Spray search radar and a passive sonobuoy processor; 60 were completed 1976-80. The HAS.2 Lynx is replacing the Wasp aboard RN destroyers and frigates. In addition to the antisubmarine role it can undertake surface attack missions armed with the new Sea Skua missile, and during the Falklands conflict it scored hits with all five missiles fired in blizzard conditions. Twenty HAS.3s, which have an uprated powerplant, have now been delivered. The French Navy variant is fitted with an Alcatel dunking sonar, and French radar and communications. Twenty six were delivered 1978-80, and a follow-up order of 14 Lynx with uprated engines was placed in 1980.

The naval Lynx has been purchased by a number of other navies for operation from frigates and destroyers built in Western Europe. The Netherlands Navy has ordered three successive batches; the first six (UH-14A) are for SAR, the second batch of ten (SH-14B) are HAS.2s with uprated engines and Alcatel dunking sonar, and the third batch of eight (SH-14C) are similar to the SH-14B but with MAD in place of the dunking sonar. The latter two types will operate from frigates of the Tromp and "Standaard" classes. The twelve Mk 88 Lynx ordered by the Federal German Navy in 1981 for the new frigates of the Bremen class are fitted with AQS-18 dunking sonar.

Above: A Lynx of the Royal Navy armed with four Sea Skua anti-ship missiles. Sea Skua was used for the first time in the South Atlantic, where it proved very successful.

Below left: A Lynx of the Brazilian Navy. Nine were purchased for operation aboard the six frigates of the Niteroi class.

Below: A Lynx UH-14A of the Netherlands Navy. Six helicopters of this type have been purchased for search and rescue (SAR).

UK
Westland Sea King

Type: (Sea King HAS.2, HAS.5) shipborne/land-based antisubmarine helicopter (crew of 4); (Sea King HC.4) shipborne commando assault helicopter (crew of 2).

Data: HAS.5.

Dimensions: Fuselage length 55ft 10in (17m); main rotor diameter 62ft (18·9m); height 16ft 10in (5·1m).

Weight: Empty (ASW) 13,672lb (6,201kg), (Commando) 12,566lb (5,700kg); maximum 21,000lb (9,525kg).

Engines: Two 1,660shp Rolls-Royce Gnome H.1400-1 free-turbine turboshafts.

Performance: Maximum speed 122kt (226km/h); service ceiling 10,000ft (3,281m); range 815nm (1,510km); mission endurance 3hr 15min.

Payload: (ASW) 2 Mk 46 or Sting ray homing torpedoes or 4 Mk 11 depth bombs; (Commando) 28 troops or 8,000lb (3,360kg) cargo.

History: First flight May 1969; service delivery (HAS.1) 1969; (HC.4) Nov 1979.

Users: UK (RN); Australia, Belgium, Egypt, FRG, India, Norway, Pakistan. ▶

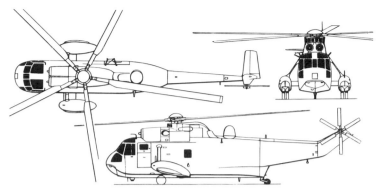

Above: Three-view of Sea King HAS.1 (HAS.5 has larger radar).

Below: A Sea King Mk 43 of the Norwegian Air Force. Ten were delivered in 1972 for search and rescue (SAR) operations. The Mk 43 has the same search radar as earlier RN models.

Above: A Sea King HC.4 of the Royal Marines lifts a Snowcat during exercises in Northern Norway.

▶The agreement to build the Sikorsky S-61 under licence was a natural continuation of earlier associations between Westland and the US company. The immediate customer was the Royal Navy, which required a large ASW helicopter to replace the Wessex. The RN's preference for rotary-over fixed-wing aircraft for the ASW role stemmed from the limited hangar capacity of the British carriers operational in the 1960s and 1970s. The Fleet Air Arm favoured independent operations, and the Sea King HAS.1 was equipped with a dunking sonar, a search radar (in a dorsal hump), doppler navigation, and an autopilot and weapon system which provided for automatic hovering at a given height or other automatic manoeuvres in all weathers. The initial RN purchase was 56 HAS.1s, built 1969-72. Twenty-one HAS.2s were ordered 1975-76, and the HAS.1s were subsequently modified to the same standard. The current RN production model is the HAS.5, which has the more powerful Sea Searcher radar, a new tactical navigation system, and passive sonobuoy dropping equipment with the associated LAPADS acoustic processing system; the dunking sonar operator monitors the LAPADS equipment at an additional crew station. Seventeen new-build HAS.5s were ordered in the late 1970s, and a further eight were ordered in 1982 following the Falklands campaign. The HAS.2s remaining in service are being brought up to the same standard. A squadron of nine HAS.2/5 Sea Kings operates from each of the Royal Navy's antisubmarine carriers, and HAS.2s are also deployed on the large support ships of the Fort Grange class. Two HAS.2s were converted to the airborne early warning (AEW) role as a result of experience in the South Atlantic. They have been fitted with the Searchwater radar which equips the Nimrod MR.2, the antenna being located in a large hinged radome which is lowered in flight and raised abreast the fuselage for take-off and landing. It is thought that a further five Sea Kings, possibly of the SAR type, will be similarly modified. Two will operate from each of the antisubmarine carriers to give warning of low-level attack. Helicopters are not particularly well-suited to the AEW mission because of their limited ceiling and the effect of vibration on radar performance, and it seems likely that the Royal Navy will investigate a longer-term solution, possibly involving tilt-rotor fixed-wing aircraft.

Above: One of four Sea King Mk 48s purchased by the Belgian Air Force for search and rescue (SAR) duties.

ASW and SAR variants of the Westland Sea King have been sold to a number of other countries. The Indian Navy will operate Sea King Mk 42s from a new class of modified Leander-class frigates, and the Australian Navy used to operate the Mk 50 from *Melbourne*. The six Mk 45s in service with the Pakistani Navy are fitted to fire AM.39 Exocet ASMs for attacks on surface vessels. The West German Marineflieger operates 22 Mk 41s in the SAR role.

The latest variant of the Westland Sea King is the HC.4 assault helicopter, a utility version of the commercially-developed Westland Commando. Fifteen HC.4s were ordered for the British Royal Marines in the late 1970s, and many of these served in 846 squadron in the South Atlantic, nine being embarked in the flagship *Hermes* on her departure from Portsmouth. Eight additional HC.4s were ordered in 1982, plus replacements for three lost in action. The Sea King HC.4 will replace the Wessex HU.5 as the standard assault helicopter of the Marines.

Below: The first of two airborne early warning (AEW) conversions of Sea King HAS.2 helicopters undertaken as a result of experience in the South Atlantic. A "Searchwater" radar developed for the Nimrod MR.2 is fitted in a large hinged radome. AEW Sea Kings first embarked on *Illustrious* in 1982.

UK
Westland Wasp

Type: (HAS.1) shipborne antisubmarine helicopter (crew of 2).
Dimensions: Fuselage length 30ft 4in (9·24m); main rotor diameter 32ft 3in (9·83m); height 11ft 8in (3·6m).
Weight: Empty 3,452lb (1,566kg); maximum 5,500lb (2,495kg).
Engines: One derated 710shp Rolls-Royce Nimbus turboshaft.
Performance: Maximum speed 104kt (193km/h); service ceiling 12,200ft (3,720m); range 263nm (488km).
Payload: 2 Mk 44/46 homing torpedoes or 2 AS.11 ASMs.
History: First flight (P.531) July 1958; (Wasp HAS.1) Oct 1962.
Users: UK (RN); Brazil, Indonesia, Netherlands, New Zealand, S. Africa.

In the late 1950s the Royal Navy investigated the possibility of operating small manned helicopters from antisubmarine frigates. The MATCH (MAnned Torpedo-Carrying Helicopter) concept envisaged using the speed of reaction and manoeuvrability of the helicopter to deliver homing torpedoes against fast-moving nuclear submarines. The helicopter chosen was the Saunders-Roe P.531, which with a more powerful engine became the Wasp. More than 70 were delivered to the Royal Navy, and the Wasp remained the standard RN light ASW helicopter until the advent of the Lynx. Some 40 Wasps were exported, notably to the Netherlands and to other navies operating frigates of British design or construction.

UK
Westland Wessex

Type: (HAS.3) shipborne antisubmarine helicopter (crew of 2); (HU.5) shipborne assault helicopter (crew of 2).
Dimensions: Fuselage length 48ft 4½in (14·74m); main rotor diameter 56ft (17·1m); height 16ft 2in (4·92m).
Weight: Empty (HAS.3) 7,850lb (3,560kg), (HU.5) 8,657lb (3,927kg); maximum (HAS.3) 12,570lb (5,700kg), (HU.5) 13,500lb (6,120kg).
Engines: (HAS.3) one 1,600shp Rolls-Royce Gazelle Mk 165 turboshaft; (HU.5) two 1,350shp Rolls-Royce Coupled Gnome Mk 110/111 turboshafts.
Performance: Maximum speed 116kt (215km/h); service ceiling 10,000-14,000ft (3,048-4,267m); range 290nm (538km).
Payload: (HAS.3) 2 Mk 44/46 homing torpedoes or 4 depth bombs; (HU.5) 12 troops or 4,000lb (1,814kg) cargo.
History: First flight (rebuilt S-58) May 1957; service delivery (HAS.1) April 1960; (HAS.3) 1966; (HU.5) Dec 1963.
Users: UK (RN); Australia.

Above: A Wasp HAS.1 antisubmarine helicopter lands on the flight deck of the frigate *Plymouth*.

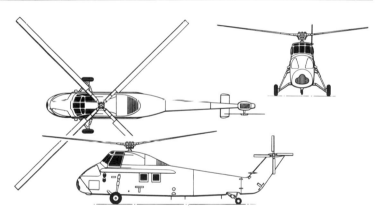

Above: Three-view of a Wessex HU.5.

Left: A Wessex HU.5 lands aboard HMS *Hermes*. The HU.5 was the Royal Navy's standard assault helicopter until the early 1980s, when it began to be replaced by the Sea King HC.4. A number of these helicopters were dragged out of retirement for the Falklands operation, serving with 845 and 848 NAS.

The Wessex is basically a Sikorsky S-58 built under licence by Westland and powered by a British turboshaft engine. Some 150 antisubmarine Wessex were built for the Royal Navy, serving aboard British carriers during the 1960s, together with 200 utility and assault versions for the RAF and the Royal Marines. The two variants which remain in service are the antisubmarine HAS.3, which is fitted with dunking sonar and operates from the remaining County class destroyers, and the HU.5 commando assault helicopter, which was used extensively during the Falklands conflict. The HAS.3 will be phased out with the County class, and the HU.5 is now being replaced by the Sea King HC.4.

Kamov Ka-25 Hormone

Type: (Hormone A) antisubmarine helicopter; (Hormone B) missile guidance helicopter; (Hormone C) SAR and utility helicopter (crew of 2 all versions).

Dimensions: Fuselage length 34ft (10·4m); main rotor diameter 51ft 8in (15·75m); height 17ft 8in (5·4m).

Weight: Empty 10,500lb (4,765kg); maximum 16,500lb (7,500kg).

Engines: Two 900hp Glushenkov GTD-3 free-turbine turboshafts.

Performance: Maximum speed 113kt (209km/h); service ceiling 11,000ft (3,350m); range 350nm (650km); mission endurance 1½-2 hours.

Payload: (Hormone A) 1-2 400mm homing torpedoes, nuclear or conventional depth bombs in internal weapons bay; maximum total load 2,200lb (1,000kg).

History: First flight (Ka-20 prototype) about 1960; service delivery (Hormone A) 1966, (Hormone B) 1967.

Users: USSR (AV-MF); India, Syria, Yugoslavia.

The Ka-25 Hormone has been the standard Soviet shipborne helicopter since it entered service in the mid-1960s, and is only now being superseded by the Ka-32 Helix. The distinctive co-axial rotor configuration characteristic of nearly all the designs emanating from the Kamov bureau results in excellent lift characteristics in a helicopter of relatively small size, although the height of the Hormone has precluded its operation from smaller surface units.

The Hormone A antisubmarine variant made its first appearance aboard the antisubmarine cruiser *Moskva* in 1967. An estimated 15-18 Ka-25s can be accommodated in a large hangar beneath the flight deck of the latter, and the

Above: A Ka-25 Hormone A antisubmarine helicopter belonging to the ASW cruiser *Kiev*. The "A" variant has a large chin radome for a search radar, a dunking sonar, towed MAD, and a weapons bay for homing torpedoes and sonobuoys. There are fuel tanks on either side of the fuselage. The box housing — not fitted on early models — may be for sonobuoys. The Hormone is now being superseded by the Ka-32 Helix, an enlarged and improved helicopter based on the Ka-25.

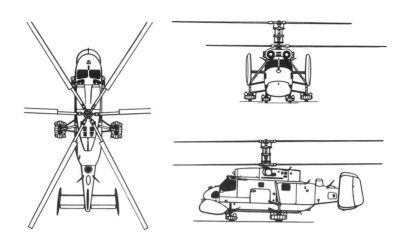

Above: Three-view of a Ka-25 Hormone A.

lifts are specially designed to accept the helicopter. The large antisubmarine ships of the Kresta II and Kara classes followed, each with a single Hormone A accommodated in a complex two-deck hangar with a lift to carry the Hormone between the hangar floor and a take-off/landing platform located above the stern. The Hormone A was subsequently operated by the Kiev class, which carries a similar number to the Moskva class, and by the "battlecruiser" *Kirov*. Five Hormone As have recently been sold to India to operate from Soviet-built destroyers of the Kashin class. The Hormone A can accommodate a variety of weapons in an internal weapons bay, and is fitted with a surface search radar (located in a prominent chin radome), a towed MAD and a dunking sonar. Fuel tanks can be fitted externally, and later models of the helicopter have a box housing on the rear fuselage which may be for sonobuoys. ▶

Below: Profile drawing of a Hormone A of the Soviet Navy. Some Hormones have the quad Yagi array depicted here, and some models have flotation bags fitted around the wheeled landing gear. This Hormone lacks the dorsal sensor found on most models, but has a radome fairing on the centre fin of the tail.

The Hormone B variant is specially fitted to provide mid-course guidance for long-range cruise missiles launched from major surface units. It has a larger chin radome (designated Puff Ball) of a different shape from that of the Hormone A, and there are a number of other differences in the electronics outfit. There appears to be no internal weapons bay. A single Hormone B helicopter is carried by the rocket cruisers of the Kresta I class and the new destroyers of the Sovremenny class, and two or three Hormone Bs are carried by the ships of the Kiev and Kirov classes.

The Hormone C is a utility helicopter, employed for plane guard and general transport duties aboard the antisubmarine cruisers of the Moskva and Kiev classes, and for vertical replenishment (VERTREP) on the large support ship *Berezina.* A reconnaissance variant, with a long ventral pannier and camera pod, has also been observed. Hormone Cs generally operate in an all-white colour-scheme which distinguishes them from other models.

Right: A Ka-25 Hormone antisubmarine helicopter lands aboard the Soviet helicopter cruiser *Moskva* in 1974. Note the large chin radome housing the search radar. The raised platform on the cruiser's flight deck is thought to have been installed for trials with the Yak-36MP Forger VTOL aircraft.

USSR
Kamov Ka-32 Helix

Type: (Helix A) shipborne antisubmarine helicopter (crew of 2?).
Dimensions: Fuselage length 37ft (11·3m); main rotor diameter 54ft 11½in (16·75m); height 18ft 0½in (5·5m).
Weight: Maximum 16,535lb (7,500kg).
Engines: Two 1,000shp Glushenkov GTD-350BM.
Performance: (Performance data can be assumed to be similar to those of the Ka-25 Hormone, with improvements in avionics, increased combat radius, and greater weapons and sonobuoy capacity.)
History: Service delivery 1981.
Users: USSR (AV-MF).

The Ka-32 Helix was first seen during exercise ZAPAD 81, when two helicopters of the type (one in civilian colours) operated from the new Soviet destroyer *Udaloy*. Although its cabin is larger than that of the Hormone, the Helix is clearly designed to be compatible with ships capable of operating the former. The antisubmarine variant which entered service on *Udaloy* has been designated Helix A, but it seems likely that "B" and "C" variants of the helicopter will also be developed for the missile guidance and utility missions respectively.

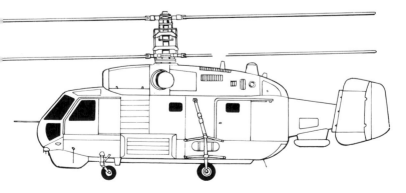

Above: A Ka-32 Helix antisubmarine helicopter on the flight deck of the new Soviet destroyer *Udaloy*. The twin hangars have telescoping roofs which slide back to accept the tall rotor head before the helicopter can be struck down.

Left: A side view of the Ka-32 Helix. The cabin is larger than that of the Hormone, and the chin radome is less prominent.

Yakovlev Yak-36MP Forger

Type: (Forger A) single-seat ship-based VTOL strike fighter.
Dimensions: Length 50ft (15·2m); span 24ft (7·3m); height 13ft 3in (4m).
Weight: Empty 16,500lb (7,485kg); maximum 25,500lb (11,565kg).
Engines: One 17,500lb (7,938kg) thrust vectored-thrust turbojet; two 8,000lb (3,630kg) thrust lift jets.
Performance: Maximum speed 630kt (1,170km/h) at altitude; service ceiling 40,000ft (12·2km); ferry range 1,566nm (2,900km); combat radius (attack) 200nm (370km), (interceptor) 100nm (185km) with 75mins loiter time.
Payload: 4 underwing pylons for 23mm cannon pods, AA-2 Atoll AAMs, drop tanks, rocket packs or AS-7 Kerry ASMs; max total load 3,000lb (1,361kg).
History: First flight 1971; service delivery 1976.
Users: USSR (AV-MF).

Above: A Yak-36MP Forger armed with four AA-2 missiles.

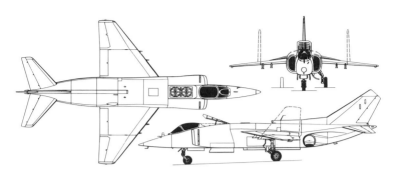

Above: Three-view of the Yak-36MP Forger.

A prototype Soviet VTOL aircraft, the YAK-36 Freehand, first went on public display in 1967. It had two turbojets side by side, with a ram inlet in the nose, exhausting through two large gridded vectored nozzles. When the production Yak-36MP finally emerged aboard the ASW cruiser *Kiev* in 1976, however, it became clear that considerable redesign work had taken place during the development phase. The Forger, like some of the abortive VTOL designs produced in Western Europe during the early 1960s, has a multi-engine configuration, with two small vertical lift jets complementing a single main vectored-thrust turbojet. The vertical lift jets improve stability in the delicate take-off and landing phases, but at the cost of higher fuel consumption (with a consequent reduction in range) and loss of the aircraft in the event of any engine failure. Moreover the multi-engine configuration precludes short rolling take-offs and the use of "ski-jump", and is therefore responsible for further limitations on payload.

The Forger appears to have been developed initially as an interceptor, to protect Soviet surface forces from air attack and to shoot down hostile reconnaissance and LRMP aircraft. However, the limited endurance and performance of the Forger, together with the lack of AEW aircraft aboard the Soviet ASW cruisers, considerably reduces its effectiveness in this role; it would be better employed as a close support aircraft, or for short-range surface strike against minor surface vessels. The Kiev-class ASW cruisers each operate a squadron of about 12 Forger As, and a number of two-seat Forger B trainers have also been observed.

Left: A Yak-36MP Forger comes in to land aboard the Soviet carrier *Minsk*. The thrust from the main engine combines with that of the two smaller lift jets to give the Forger stability during the take-off and landing phases. Note the louvred door immediately behind the cockpit for the two lift jets; these are disposed vertically and in tandem.

Bell AH-1 SeaCobra

Type: (AH-1J, AH-1T) shipborne ground support helicopter (crew of 2).
Data: AH-1J.
Dimensions: Fuselage length 44ft 7in (13·6m); main rotor diameter 44ft (13·4m); height 13ft 8in (4·17m).
Weight: Empty 7,261lb (3,294kg); maximum 10,000lb (4,536kg).
Engines: One 1,800shp Pratt & Whitney Aircraft of Canada T400-CP-400 twin-turboshaft.
Performance: Maximum speed 180kt (333km/h); service ceiling 10,550ft (3,215m); range 310nm (575km); mission endurance 2 hours.
Payload: 1 20mm XM-197 3-barrel gun in electrically-driven undernose turret; 4 stores attachment points under stub wings for gun/rocket pods.
History: First flight (prototype) 1969; service delivery (AH-1J) 1970, (AH-1T) Oct 1977.
Users: US Marine Corps.

The SeaCobra is a specialised gunship helicopter derived from the Huey series. It has a particularly narrow frontal aspect, the crew of two being seated in tandem. A triple-barrelled gun turret is fitted beneath the nose, and there are stub wings for gun pods or rocket packs. The initial US Marine Corps order was for the single-engine AH-1G, but from 1970 to 1975 69 of the improved AH-1J model were delivered. These served in three attack helicopter squadrons each of 18 AH-1G/J. The AH-1T is now in production, and 57 will be procured to replace the AH-1Gs and to increase squadron strength to 24 units. The AH-1T is larger, has a single more powerful engine (the 1,970shp T400-WV-402) and a bigger payload, which will eventually include the TOW anti-tank missile. A handful of the 202 TOW-capable Ah-1J SeaCobras supplied to Iran under a 1972 contract saw action in 1980-81 during the war against Iraq. Most are currently immobilised.

Bell UH-1N Iroquois

Type: shipborne utility helicopter (crew of 1).
Dimensions: Fuselage length 42ft 5in (12·9m); main rotor diameter 48ft 2in (14·7m); height 14ft 10¼in (4·53m).
Weight: Empty 6,143lb (2,787kg); maximum 11,200lb (5,080kg).
Engines: One 1,800shp Pratt & Whitney Aircraft of Canada PT6T-3B coupled turboshaft.
Performance: Maximum speed 124kt (230km/h); service ceiling 14,200ft (4,430m); range 227nm (420km).

Above: A UH-1N Iroquois of VXE-6, the Antarctic development squadron. The red paint-scheme contrasts with the ice.

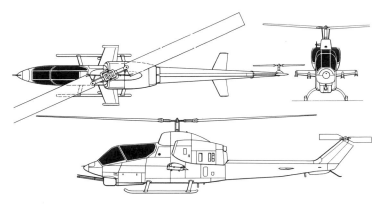

Above: Three-view of an AH-1J SeaCobra.

Above: An AH-1J SeaCobra of the US Marines. The turreted 20mm 3-barrel cannon is used for ground support.

Payload: 14 passengers, or 3,383lb (1,534kg) cargo externally.
History: First flight 1968; service delivery (UH-1N) 1971.
Users: US Marine Corps, US Navy; Norway, Peru, Thailand.

The name "Huey" by which this helicopter is generally known derives from the HU-1 designation conferred on early models of the Iroquois. A total of 225 improved UH-1Ns were delivered to the US Navy and US Marine Corps 1971-78. The Marine Corps operates three squadrons each of 24 helicopters, detachments generally being embarked aboard LPHs and LHAs on deployment. The Navy uses the UH-1N in conjunction with the H-46 Sea Knight and SH-3G Sea King in helicopter combat support squadrons.

Above: A UH-1N utility helicopter of the US Navy. The "Huey" is the standard liaison helicopter of the US Navy and USMC.

USA
Boeing-Vertol H-46
Sea Knight

Type: (CH-46) shipborne assault helicopter (crew of 3); (UH-46) shipborne replenishment helicopter.
Data: CH-46E.
Dimensions: Fuselage length 44ft 10in (13·66m); main rotor diameter 51ft (15·6m); height 16ft 8in (5·1m).
Weight: Empty 13,112lb (5,948kg); maximum 23,000lb (10,433kg).
Engines: Two 1,870shp General Electric T58-16 turboshafts.
Performance: Maximum speed 143kt (265km/h); service ceiling 14,000ft (4,267m); range 206nm (381·5km).
Payload: 17 troops or 10,000lb (4,535kg) cargo.
History: First flight (prototype CH-46A) Aug 1959; service delivery (CH-46A) 1964; (CH-46D) 1966; (CH-46E) 1977.
Users: US Navy, US Marine Corps.

The CH-46 Sea Knight is the standard assault helicopter of the US Marine Corps. The twin-rotor configuration results in a long, broad cabin in which 17 fully-armed combat troops can be seated. The troops embark and disembark via a rear-loading ramp.

Six hundred and twenty-four CH-46As were built during the early 1960s, and these were followed by the improved CH-46D variant. The CH-46D, delivered from 1966 onwards, was given more powerful 1,400shp engines and cambered rotor blades, and later models had additional electronics. The US Marine Corps has 12 medium helicopter squadrons operating CH-46A/D Sea Knights, each with 12 or 18 helicopters. Two hundred and seventy-three of these are being brought up to CH-46E standard under a modernisation programme which began in 1977. Modifications include the fitting of uprated T58-GE-16 engines (1,870shp), a crash- and combat-resistant fuel system, and an improved navigation system.

The UH-46 is the US Navy's standard vertical replenishment (VERTREP) helicopter, and operates alongside UH-1 Hueys and SH-53G Sea Kings in four helicopter combat support squadrons. Twenty-four UH-46As (based on the CH-46A) were delivered from 1964 onwards, and these were superseded by the UH-46D (based on the CH-46D) in September 1966. Many of the large auxiliary support vessels built by the US Navy during the 1960s have fixed hangar and maintenance facilities aft, and operate two or three UH-46s for the transfer of dry stores.

Below: US Marines board a CH-46 Sea Knight on an amphibious assault ship. Troops embark and disembark via a rear-loading ramp, with an alternative loading of 10,000lb of cargo for the support/replenishment role.

Right: The CH-46 Sea Knight has been the standard medium-lift helicopter in the US Marine Corps since the early 1960s. A modernisation programme has been underway since 1977 to prolong service life.

USA
Grumman A-6 Intruder

Type: (A-6E) two-seat carrier-based all-weather attack aircraft; (KA-6D) two-seat refuelling tanker aircraft.
Data: A-6E.
Dimensions: Length 54ft 9in (16·69m); span 53ft (16·15m); height 16ft 2in (4·93m).
Weight: Empty 26,660lb (12,093kg); maximum 60,400lb (27,397kg).
Engines: Two 9,300lb (4,218kg) thrust Pratt & Whitney J52-8A two-shaft turbojets.
Performance: Maximum speed 563kt (1,043km/h) at sea level; service ceiling 42,500ft (12,995m); range (max external fuel) 2,818nm (5,222km); unrefuelled combat radius 300nm (556km).
Payload: 5 stores pylons each rated at 3,600lb (1,633kg) for ASMs, bombs and rockets; maximum total payload of 18,000lb (8,165kg).
History: First flight (prototype) April 1960; service delivery (A-6A) Feb 1963; first flight (KA-6D) May 1966; (A-6E) Feb 1970.
Users: US Navy, US Marine Corps.

The A-6 Intruder was designed from the outset as an all-weather medium attack aircraft. It is fitted with the DIANE (Digital Integrated Attack Navigation

Below: An A-6E of VA-65 "Tigers" belonging to the carrier *Dwight D. Eisenhower* (CVN-69). The protrusion under the nose is for TRAM (Target Recognition Attack Multisensor), an electro-optical system designed to permit the Intruder to make blind precision attacks. The five weapons pylons can accommodate a wide variety of ordnance, and the prominent nose probe, which allows refuelling by KA-6D tanker conversions, enables the Intruder to strike at long range. The Intruder's capabilities are now being further enhanced by the introduction of the Harpoon ASM and HARM anti-radiation missile.

Equipment) system, which enables the entire flight mission to be flown without visual reference.

The model in current service with the US Navy and the Marine Corps is the A-6E, which introduced a new multi-mode radar and a new computer. A total of 159 new-build A-6Es were purchased, and a further 240 A-6As were modified to the same standard. The A-6E has been constantly updated, the latest addition being TRAM (Target Recognition Attack Multisensor), a turreted electro-optical system designed for use in blind precision attack, if necessary with laser-guided weapons. Intruders are currently being modified to fire the Harpoon anti-ship missile, the first Harpoon-capable aircraft being deployed in 1981, and a programme to integrate the HARM anti-radiation missile with the Intruder is now underway.

The Intruder serves in 12 active US Navy medium attack squadrons, each squadron comprising ten A-6Es plus a detachment of four KA-6D tanker aircraft. Mid-flight refuelling enables strikes to be carried out at a range well beyond that of the A-7 Corsair. The Marine Corps operates five medium attack squadrons each with 12 A-6Es. It was thought that construction of the Intruder would terminate in the late 1970s, but the absence of a projected replacement aircraft capable of undertaking the same missions has resulted in a prolonged production run in order to maintain the active squadrons at current levels.

Below: A Bullpup ASM is fired by an A-6A Intruder.

Grumman EA-6 Prowler

Type: (EA-6A and EA-6B) two/four-seat electronic countermeasures aircraft.
Data: EA-6B.
Dimensions: Length 59ft 5in (18·1m); span 53ft (16·15m); height 16ft 3in (4·95m).
Weight: Empty 32,162lb (14,588kg); maximum 65,100lb (29,530kg).
Engines: Two 11,200lb (5,080kg) thrust Pratt & Whitney J52-408 two-shaft turbojets.
Performance: Maximum speed 566kt (1,048km/h) at sea level; service ceiling (five pods) 38,000ft (11,582m); range 2,085nm (3,861km); combat radius (five pods) 470nm (870km).
History: First flight (EA-6A) 1963; (EA-6B) May 1968; service delivery (EA-6B) Jan 1971.
Users: US Navy, US Marine Corps.

The value of integrating electronic warfare aircraft into the carrier air wings was demonstrated in the Vietnam War, when strikes frequently had to be mounted against targets heavily defended by batteries of surface-to-air missiles. The first attempt to provide a specialist ECM aircraft for the US Navy was the EA-6A Intruder, a converted A-6A fitted with more than 30 different antennae for monitoring, classifying, recording, jamming and deceiving enemy radar transmissions, but which retained a limited attack capability. The EA-6B Prowler which succeeded it is, however, a completely redesigned aircraft incorporating a very advanced and comprehensive suite of ECM equipment, both internal and podded. Five ALQ-99 high-power tactical jamming pods, each with windmill generators to supply their power requirements, can be carried, and enemy radar transmissions are monitored and countered by two EW operators seated side by side in the rear. The pilot sits on the left, and on his right is an ECM officer who manages navigation, communications, defensive ECM and the dispensing of chaff. The change from a two-seat to a four-seat configuration has entailed a complete redesign of the forward part of the fuselage, resulting in a longer aircraft than the baseline A-6.

The US Navy has nine electronic warfare squadrons currently in service, each of four aircraft, and construction continues with a view to providing one squadron for each of the carrier air wings. EA-6Bs also serve alongside older EA-6As in a single Marine Corps ECM squadron.

Above: EA-6A (top) and EA-6B of VMAQ-2. The Marine Corps operates one ECM squadron.

Below: Each ALQ-99 tactical jamming pod is powered by a windmill generator.

USA
Grumman E-2C Hawkeye

Type: (E-2B,C) airborne early warning and air control (crew of 5).
Dimensions: Length 57ft 7in (17·55m); span 80ft 7in (24·56m); height 18ft 4in (5·6m).
Weight: Empty 37,945lb (17,211kg); maximum 51,817lb (23,503kg).
Engines: Two 4,910shp Allison T56-425 turboprops.
Performance: Maximum speed 326kt (604km/h) service ceiling 30,800ft (9,390m); ferry range 1,394nm (2,583km); radius 200nm (370km) with six hours on station.
History: First flight (E-2A) April 1961; (E-2B) Feb 1969; (E-2C) Jan 1971.
Users: US Navy; Japan.

The most capable carrier-based airborne early warning (AEW) aircraft yet produced, the E-2C Hawkeye has been offered as an alternative to the more expensive E-3 AWACS to operate from land bases, and a number of aircraft of this type have been purchased by Israel and Japan. In its naval application the E-2C is stationed some 200nm (370km) from the carrier, using its height above sea level to extend the radar horizon of the task force. Hostile aircraft are tracked and fighters of the combat air patrol (CAP) vectored out towards them; the E-2C can also pick up hostile surface units before they enter missile range and direct carrier attack aircraft against them. The key to the aircraft's mission is the distinctive 24ft (7·3m) diameter saucer-shaped radome for the APS-125 UHF radar, which is mounted above the fuselage. The dome rotates in a free airstream at six revolutions per minute, and can be retracted for hangar stowage aboard the older carriers, reducing height to 16ft (4·87m). The radar can pick up aircraft up to 240nm (444km) away and can track 250 air and surface targets simultaneously. Data are analysed by an on-board computer and the radar picture monitored by three controllers seated at consoles in the Combat Information Centre (CIC), which is located in the fuselage directly beneath the radome. The Airborne Tactical Data System (ATDS) incorporates data links providing real-time communications with the task force or land base. A production run of 95 aircraft for the US Navy is due to be completed in 1986. This will provide enough aircraft for a four-plane detachment for each of the carrier air wings.

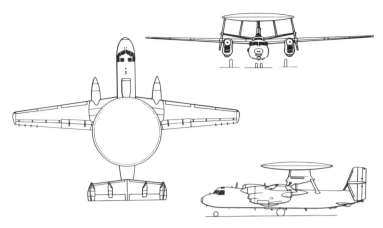

Above: Three-view of an E-2C Hawkeye.

Above: An E-2 Hawkeye from a training unit practises landing on a carrier. E-2B models continued to serve in first-line squadrons until recently, but it is planned to replace these by the E-2C model, which has more advanced electronics, in the near future. A total production run of 95 E-2Cs is envisaged.

Left: Overhead view of an E-2C Hawkeye. The distinctive saucer-shaped radome houses the APS-125 UHF radar, which rotates in a free airstream at six revolutions per minute. The Hawkeye provides not only detection of hostile forces at extended ranges, but command and control of the air-space around the carrier. It can handle and control more than 30 individual interceptions of hostile aircraft.

USA
Grumman F-14 Tomcat

Type: (F-14A, F-14C) two-seat carrier-based fleet air defence fighter.
Data: F-14A.
Dimensions: Length 62ft 8in (19·1m); span (68° sweep) 38ft 2in (11·63m), (20° sweep) 64ft 1½in (19·54m); height 16ft (4·88m).
Weight: Empty 39,762lb (18,036kg); normal 58,539lb (26,553kg); maximum 74,348lb (33,724kg).
Engines: Two 20,900lb (9,480kg) thrust Pratt & Whitney TF30-412A two-shaft afterburning turbofans.
Performance: Maximum speed 1,359kt (2,517km/h) at altitude, 794kt (1,470km/h) at sea level; service ceiling 56,000ft (17,070m); range 2,000nm (3,704km); combat radius 500nm (926km).
Payload: 1 20mm M61-A1 Vulcan multi-barrel cannon in fuselage; 6 AIM-54 Phoenix and 2 AIM-9 Sidewinder AAMs or 4 AIM-7 Sparrow and 4 AIM-9; maximum total load 14,500lb (6,577kg).
History: First flight Dec 1970; initial deployment US Navy Oct 1972.
Users: US Navy.

The F-14 Tomcat is the world's most advanced carrier-based fighter. Designed for the Fleet Air Defence role, the Tomcat would operate round-the clock combat air patrols in conjunction with the E-2C Hawkeye airborne early warning aircraft. A Hawkeye would be stationed some 200nm (370km) from its carrier in the direction of an expected attack, while detachments of Tomcats would patrol a sector some 50nm (93km) closer to the carrier, ready to be vectored out to intercept incoming bombers. The powerful AWG-9 doppler-pulse fire control radar, which is mounted in the nose of the F-14, can track simultaneously up to 24 targets, plus its own missiles, out to a distance of 60-100nm (111-185km) using track-while-scan techinques. The Phoenix air-to-air missile, unique to this aircraft, incorporates an auto-pilot set by the

Below: An F-14A Tomcat of VF-142 "Ghostriders" belonging to the carrier *Dwight D. Eisenhower* (CVN 69). The low-contrast grey paint scheme has replaced the more flamboyant schemes applied to Tomcats in the late 1970s. All of the more modern US carriers now operate the F-14A in place of the McDonnell Douglas F-4 Phantom.

Right: An F-14A Tomcat with two AIM-7 Sparrow and two AIM-9 Sidewinder missiles on the underwing pylons. Sparrow is a medium-range semi-active missile which has to be guided by the Tomcat's own AWG-9 fire control radar; Sidewinder is a heat-seeking "fire-and-forget" missile, making it better suited to dogfights.

fire control system as the missile is fired. The target is illuminated only when the missile approaches its target, making countermeasures difficult. Besides its semi-active homing head the missile also incorporates a short-range active radar, so that beyond a certain point the missile homes itself. The only limitation on this very capable system — and on other systems employing semi-active homing — is that all targets must be in the field of vision of the radar, and the F-14 must therefore be kept pointed at the target. Shorter-range infra-red homing (Sidewinder) missiles are also carried for close engagements, and there is a single multi-barrel Vulcan M61 20mm cannon. The adoption of variable geometry gives good close combat manoeuvrability. The angle of the wings is computer-controlled to obtain the best possible performance in a combat situation; the wings extend for slow-speed landings and long-range flight and retract for high-speed manoeuvring.

The F-14 has a very advanced airframe which employs canted vertical tailplanes above each engine; the tailplane skins are of boron epoxy composite. Problems were experienced in the early stages of the aircraft's operational life with the engines, the fuselage structure and the computer weapon system. Many of these problems, and in particular that of the fuselage structure (which admitted water with attendant corrosion problems) have now been ironed out, but it is still generally accepted that the Tomcat is underpowered. It was intended early in the programme that the main production run would be the F-14B, which would have the more powerful F401 turbofan, but this was not proceeded with because of rocketing costs which threatened to leave the US Navy short of the numbers it required. More than 460 Tomcats had been delivered to the Navy by early 1983, and current plans envisage the construction of sufficient aircraft for 24 squadrons (there are at present 18). Eighty additional aircraft were purchased by Iran, but a programme to equip the US Marine Corps with the aircraft was cancelled in 1975.

Two squadrons each of 12 Tomcats are operated by each of the newer US Navy super-carriers, and since 1981 these have included a detachment of ▶

▶ specially-fitted F-14A/TARPS photo-reconnaissance aircraft. The F-14A has replaced the RF-8G Crusader in this role, and carries frame and panoramic cameras and an infra-red line scanner in a pod mounted beneath the fuselage (i.e. in place of the Phoenix missiles); this podded system is designated TARPS (Tactical Air Reconnaissance Pod System). The aircraft so fitted can be easily converted to the ''straight'' fighter role. From late 1983 the standard production aircraft will be the F-14C with numerous avionic updates including advanced electronic displays in both cockpits, new radar and programmable processor, laser-gyro INS, ASPJ (Advanced Self-Protection Jammer) and the JTIDS (Joint Tactical Information Distribution System).

Right: Three-view of an F-14A Tomcat.

Below: A Tomcat of VF-84 "Jolly Rogers" is catapulted from the angled deck of *Nimitz* (CVN 68), while a second Tomcat of VF-41 "Black Aces" awaits its turn on the port forward catapult. The photograph was taken while *Nimitz* was participating in the NATO exercise TEAMWORK 80 off Northern Norway. These aircraft hold the key to the US Navy's ability to operate in Northern waters against the threat from the Soviet bombers such as the Tu-22M Backfire.

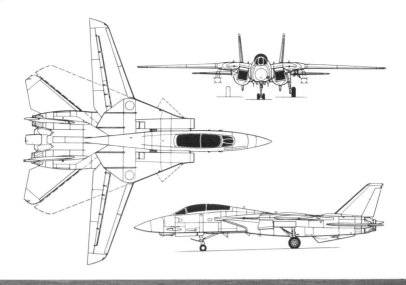

Grumman S-2 Tracker

Type: (Variants: see text) four-seater carrier-/land based antisubmarine and patrol aircraft.
Data: S-2E.
Dimensions: Length 43ft 6in (13·26m); span 72ft 7in (22·13m); height 16ft 7in (5·06m).
Weight: Empty 18,750lb (8,505kg); maximum 29,150lb (13,222kg).
Engines: Two 1,525hp Wright R-1820-82WA Cyclone nine-cylinder radials.
Performance: Maximum speed 230kt (426km/h) at sea level; service ceiling 21,000ft (6,400m); range 1,130nm (2,095km).
Payload: 2 homing torpedoes, 2 Mk 101 depth bombs or 4 385lb (175kg) depth charges in internal weapons bay; 6 underwing pylons for bombs or rockets.
History: First flight (prototype) Dec 1952; (S-2A) 1953; final delivery Feb 1968.
Users: Argentina, Australia, Brazil, Canada, Italy, Japan, Peru, South Korea, Taiwan, Thailand, Turkey, Uruguay, Venezuela.

The S-2 Tracker was designed as a carrier aircraft capable of both ASW search and ASW strike. These roles had previously been undertaken by pairs of aircraft — Guardians or Skyraiders — one of which carried the detection systems and the other the weapons. Development proceeded rapidly in spite of the need to accommodate a much wider variety of equipment than had hitherto been possible, and the long wing-span of the Tracker resulted in excellent handling characteristics. The pilot and co-pilot sit side-by-side beneath a broad canopy, with two systems operators behind them. The search radar is in a retractable ventral bin, an extendable MAD boom is located in the tail, and the engine nacelles carry sonobuoys which are ejected from tubes in the rear. The transfer of US Navy fixed-wing ASW squadrons from escort carriers to the Essex-class fleet carriers in the late 1950s resulted in the larger S-2D and S-2E variants, of which 1,281 were built. The S-2E was given a more capacious weapons bay, a new search radar, computerised ASW equipment, and provision for the Julie-Jezebel active-passive explosive echoranging system.

Right: An S-2F Tracker of the Thai Navy. Following the demise of the Essex-class antisubmarine carriers (CVS) of the US Navy in the early 1970s, large numbers of Trackers were refurbished for sale to other countries. Most of these countries now operate them from shore bases for ASW duties. Ten such aircraft are in service with the Thai Navy which employs the S-2 also as a maritime patrol and general reconnaissance platform.

Above: An S-2G Tracker of the Australian Navy is lined up on the catapult of the carrier _Melbourne_. With the demise of the latter the S-2E/Gs will have to operate from shore bases.

The Tracker was less well-suited to operation from the new super-carriers, which were built without AVGAS stowage, and its effective range was limited by the need for a carrier-borne command and control system. It was therefore succeeded in US Navy service by the jet-propelled S-3 Viking. A large number of Tracker aircraft — principally the A, E, and F variants — were purchased by other countries, and the S-2 is still operated by the Brazilian and Argentinian Navies from the decks of their fleet carriers. The S-2s once operated from Australian, Canadian and Dutch carriers are now employed in land-based ASW/patrol/reconnaissance roles.

Left: A S-2F Tracker of the Japanese Maritime Self-Defense Force. The retractable radome beneath the fuselage is for a search radar, and the lengthened engine nacelles carry sonobuoys. Bombs or rockets are carried on six underwing pylons. 21 S-2Fs were purchased by Japan, but a number of these are now in mothballs, and the others will probably follow shortly. The type is being superseded in JMSDF service by the P-3 Orion.

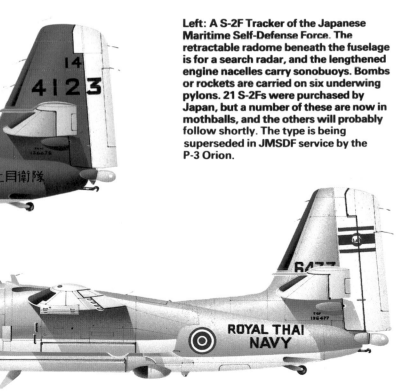

USA

Kaman SH-2 Seasprite

Type: (SH-2F) shipborne antisubmarine helicopter (crew of 3).
Data: SH-2F.
Dimensions: Fuselage length 40ft 6in (12·3m); main rotor diameter 44ft (13·4m); height 13ft 7in (4·14m).
Weight: Empty 7,040lb (3,193kg); maximum 12,800lb (5,806kg).
Engines: Two 1,350shp General Electric T58-8F turboshafts.
Performance: Maximum speed 143kt (265km/h); service ceiling 22,500ft (6,858m); range (max fuel) 367nm (679km); mission endurance 2½ hours.
Payload: 2 Mk 46 homing torpedoes.
History: First flight (prototype) July 1959; service delivery (UH-2A) Dec 1962; (SH-2D) 1972; (SH-2F) Sept 1973.

The SH-2 Seasprite is the US Navy's current LAMPS (Light Airborne Multi-Purpose System) helicopter, and operates in that role from cruisers of the CG-26 class, from destroyers of the DD-963 and DDG-993 classes, and from frigates of the FF-1042, FF-1052, FFG-1 and FFG-7 classes. Many of these vessels were initially designed to operate DASH anti-submarine drones (see Introduction), but with the failure of the DASH programme it was decided to modify UH-2D utility and HH-2D SAR helicopters for antisubmarine warfare and anti-missile defence, and to extend hangar facilities on the frigates to accommodate them. The LAMPS I configuration involved the fitting of two tons of special equipment, including a powerful chin search radar, sonobuoys, ASQ-81 MAD, ECM and new avionics. The first of 20 SH-2D conversions flew in March 1971, the full order being completed in 12 months; evaluation took place aboard the CG-26 class with conspicuous success. Deliveries of the first of 87 improved SH-2F conversions began in September 1973; modifications included a new rotor, improved sensors, and a higher gross weight. All remaining SH-2Ds are being upgraded to "F" standard.

SH-2D/F Seasprites currently make up six US Navy light antisubmarine helicopter squadrons providing detachments to surface ships, plus two training squadrons. They are to be superseded by the SH-60B Seahawk (LAMPS III) aboard the DD-963, DDG-993 and FFG-7 classes, but will continue to operate from the older vessels, which have hangars too small to accommodate the new helicopter. Because of this 48 new SH-2Fs have recently been ordered.

Below: All LAMPS I helicopters in service with the US Navy have now been updated to SH-2F configuration, with low-vibration rotor, uprated engines, repositioned tailwheel and improved electronics. This particular Seasprite belongs to the ASW frigate *Valdez* (FF 1096). Note chin mounted surveillance radar.

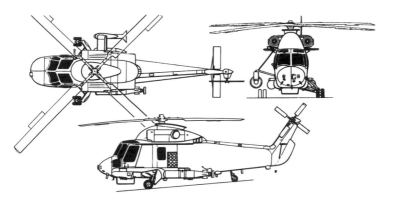

Above: Three-view of an SH-2F Seasprite.

Above: An SH-2F antisubmarine helicopter releases a sonobuoy. Data is processed by the mother-ship, which then directs the helicopter to attack with homing torpedoes.

USA
Lockheed S-3 Viking

Type: (S-3A, S-3B) four-seat carrier-based antisubmarine aircraft.
Dimensions: Length 53ft 4in (16·26m); span 68ft 8in (20·93m); height 22ft 9in (6·93m).
Weight: Empty 26,783lb (12,149kg); maximum 52,539lb (23,832kg).
Engines: Two 9,275lb (4,207kg) thrust General Electric TF34-400 two-shaft turbofans.
Performance: Maximum speed 440kt (814km/h) at sea level; service ceiling 35,000ft (10,670m); ferry range 3,000nm (5,556km); mission range 2,000nm (3,705km); mission endurance 9 hours.
Payload: 2/4 Mk 46 homing torpedoes, 2/4 depth bombs in internal weapons bays; two wing pylons for Harpoon missiles, bombs, rockets or fuel tanks.
History: First flight Jan 1972; service delivery Oct 1973.
Users: US Navy.

Designed to replace the venerable S-2 Tracker in the carrier-borne fixed-wing antisubmarine role, the S-3 Viking is an altogether more sophisticated aircraft equipped with the most advanced detection and data processing capabilities. The major proportion of the Viking's cost is taken up by electronics. Sensors include a high-resolution radar (APS-116), MAD (AQS-81), Forward-Looking Infra-Red (FLIR), and a tube launcher for 60 sonobuoys. The MAD boom, FLIR, and the fuel probe retract into the fuselage to reduce drag. Sensor data are processed by a 65,000-word AYK-30 digital computer. Behind the pilot and co-pilot, seated side-by-side beneath a broad cockpit, there are consoles for a tactical coordinator and a systems operator.

The initial US Navy production run of 184 aircraft was completed in FY1977. From the mid-1970s fixed-wing ASW squadrons (VS) each of ten S-3A Vikings were added to the air groups of the US super-carriers. Only the two older carriers of the Midway class do not operate the Viking. In spite of some initial criticism directed at the additional maintenance load imposed by the S-3A, its ability to react quickly and effectively to a distant submarine contact has proved invaluable, and a contract has recently been signed for the upgrading of 160 S-3As to S-3B standard; the latter modification will involve an increase in acoustic and radar processing capabilities, expanded ESM coverage, a new sonobuoy receiver system, and the Harpoon anti-ship missile. "Harpooning" the Viking will meet another criticism of the aircraft made by traditional carrier aviators, who feel that the embarkation of fixed-wing ASW aircraft has compromised the concept of the attack carrier, and reduced its striking power.

Above: An S-3A Viking of VS-41 "Shamrocks", the shore-based squadron which handles all S-3A readiness training. All except the two oldest carriers of the Midway class now operate a squadron of ten Vikings for long-range ASW patrol. The prosecution of submarine contacts in the vicinity of the task force is the responsibility of Sea King ASW helicopters.

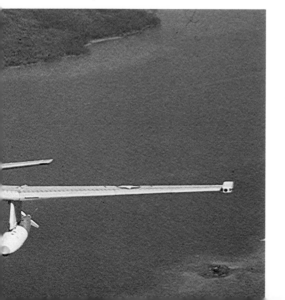

Left: An S-3A Viking of VS-29 "Vikings" belonging to the Forrestal-class carrier *Ranger* (CV 61). Not all US aviators are happy about the assignment of squadrons of fixed-wing ASW aircraft to attack carriers, but the threat of Soviet submarines armed with long-range missiles (SSGNs) makes the Viking an essential part of the modern carrier air wing.

McDonnell Douglas A-4 Skyhawk

Type: (Variants: see text) single-seat carrier-/land-based light attack aircraft.
Data: A-4M.
Dimensions: Length 40ft 3¼in (12·3m); span 27ft 6in (8·38m); height 15ft (4·57m).
Weight: Empty 10,465lb (4,747kg); maximum (carrier-based) 24,500lb (11,113kg), (land-based) 27,420lb (12,437kg).
Engines: One 11,200lb (5,080kg) thrust Pratt & Whitney J52-408A turbojet.
Performance: Maximum speed 560kt (1,040km/h) at sea level; service ceiling 49,000ft (14,935m); range 1,785nm (3,306km); combat radius 335nm (620km).
Payload: 2 20mm Colt Mk 12 cannon; pylons for maximum total load of 9,155lb (4,135kg).
History: First flight June 1954; squadron delivery (A-4A) Oct 1956; (A-4M) April 1970; (A-4N) June 1972.
Users: US Marine Corps; Argentina, Australia.

Affectionately known as "Heinemann's hot-rod" after its designer, Ed. Heinemann, the A-4 Skyhawk began life as a lightweight day nuclear strike aircraft operating from US Navy carriers. Its small size — the early versions had a take-off weight only half that of the original US Navy requirement (30,000lb, 13,610kg) — was made possible by the elimination of virtually all electronic equipment. The wing was constructed as a single unit with an integral fuel tank, a folding wing being unnecessary because of the small size of the Skyhawk. Later versions were heavier due to the installation of more powerful engines, and increases in fuel capacity and payload. All-weather avionics were added in a distinctive dorsal "hump" from the A-4F onwards. The last model to be built in large numbers was the A-4M. In all 2,960 Skyhawks were built, and the aircraft continued in production for the US Marine Corps until 1979.

The Skyhawk was replaced by the A-7 Corsair aboard the US Navy's super-carriers in the late 1960s, but was retained aboard the older carriers of the

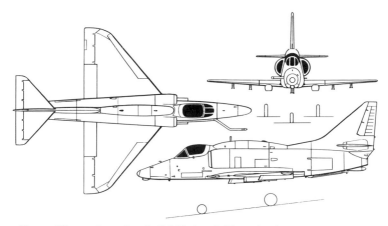

Above: Three-view of an A-4M Skyhawk. Note the dorsal hump.

Essex class until *Hancock* decommissioned in 1975. It is now used by the Navy only for training, but the Marine Corps still has four light attack squadrons (VMA) each with 19 A-4Ms; these will be replaced in the near future by the AV-8B Harrier II. Seventy A-4P Skyhawks (converted A-4B/C) were purchased by the Argentine Air Force from 1966 onwards and were employed extensively on maritime strike missions during the Falklands conflict of 1982. The Argentine Navy also purchased 16 A-4Q Skyhawks in 1971 for operation from the carrier *25 de Mayo*. The Australian Navy purchased eight new A-4G Skyhawks in 1967 for the carrier *Melbourne*, and a similar number of ex-US A-4Gs in 1971.

Below: An A-4M Skyhawk of light attack squadron VMA-214. At present there are four Marine light attack squadrons with Skyhawks, and a further three with the AV-8A Harrier. Skyhawks remain in service with a number of other countries, notably Argentina and Australia, although with the decommissioning of *Melbourne* RAN A-4s are now land-based.

USA (UK)
McDonnell Douglas (BAe)
AV-8 Harrier

Type: (AV-8A/C, AV-8B, AV-8S Matador) single-seat ship-/land-based tactical attack aircraft.
Data: AV-8A.
Dimensions: Length 45ft 6in (13·9m); span 25ft 3in (7·7m); height 11ft 3in (3·4m).
Weight: Empty 12,200lb (5,533kg); maximum over 25,000lb (11,340kg).
Engines: One 21,500lb (9,752kg) thrust Rolls-Royce Pegasus 103 two-shaft vectored-thrust turbofan.
Performance: Maximum speed 640kt (1,185km/h) at low level; service ceiling 50,000ft (15,240m); range with maximum fuel 1,600nm (2,965km); combat radius (attack) 200nm (370km), (fighter) 400nm (740km).
Payload: 2 30mm Aden cannon gun pods; 2 AIM-9 Sidewinder AAMs; 3 1,000lb (454kg) or 5 500lb (227kg) bombs; maximum total load 5,950lb (2,700kg).
History: First flight (development Harrier) Aug 1966; service delivery (GR.1) April 1969; (AV-8A) 1971.
Users: US Marine Corps; Spain.

Developed from the experimental P.1127 Kestrel, the Harrier first entered service with the British Royal Air Force as a close support aircraft (GR.1) operating from unprepared fields. The US Marine Corps showed a keen interest in the aircraft, which flew test flights from several US ships before its adoption in the late 1960s for the beach assault mission, with a subsidiary defensive role. One hundred and ten AV-8A Harriers, based on the RAF's GR.3 but modified to Marine Corps specifications, were built in the UK under contract from McDonnell Douglas between 1971 and 1977. In 1975 Spain ordered six AV-8Ss (re-christened *Matador*) plus two TAV-8S trainers for VTOL operations from the carrier *Dédalo*, and a further five were delivered in 1980.

Right: A prototype AV-8B Harrier II (near camera) flies alongside an AV-8A of the US Marine Corps. The AV-8B represents a tremendous advance on its predecessor. Payload has been trebled by adopting a supercritical wing with advanced wing characteristics. The AV-8B has a raised cockpit similar to that of the Sea Harrier, thereby increasing the space available for avionics. 336 AV-8Bs are planned for the USMC. They will begin to replace the A-4M Skyhawk and the AV-8A Harrier in the Marine light attack squadrons from 1985 onwards and will also serve with the Spanish Navy and, as the GR.5, with the Royal Air Force.

Above: Eleven AV-8S Matadors plus two TAV-8S trainers have been delivered to the Spanish Navy for the carrier *Dédalo*.

The Marine Corps aircraft differed from their RAF counterparts in being fitted from the outset to carry AIM-9 Sidewinder AAMs on the outer pylons for the air defence role, and it was the Marines who introduced the practice of VIFFing (=vectoring in forward flight) in close combat. The best 47 USMC aircraft have been converted to AV-8C standard with updated EW systems, flare/chaff dispenser, a lift-improvement system, new communications and on board oxygen generation. Detachments of AV-8A Harriers operate regularly from the Tarawa-class LHAs, and have also operated experimentally from the LPH *Guam* (the interim Sea Control Ship 1972-74) and the CVA *Franklin D. Roosevelt* (Mediterranean 1976-77). The employment of a short rolling take-off, vertical landing (STOVL) mode of operations enables more than 5,000lb (2,270kg) of bombs to be carried. This figure will be trebled in the new AV-8B, which has a supercritical wing with greatly improved lift characteristics. Two hundred and fifty-seven AV-8Bs are to be acquired by the Marine Corps beginning in FY1982, against a long-term requirement for 336; the AV-8B will replace the AV-8A/C and the A-4M Skyhawk in Marine attack squadrons. The aircraft has also been ordered by the RAF as the GR.5.

McDonnell Douglas F/A-18 Hornet

Type: (F/A-18A) single-seat carrier-/land-based multi-role fighter.
Dimensions: Length 56ft (17·07m); span 37ft 6in (11·42m); height 15ft 4in (4·7m).
Weight: Empty 23,939lb (10,859kg); maximum (fighter role) 33,585lb (15,235kg), (attack role) 48,253lb (21,887kg).
Engines: Two 16,000lb (7,257kg) thrust General Electric F404-400 two-shaft augmented turbofans.
Performance: Maximum speed 1,034kt (1,915km/h) at altitude; service ceiling 49,000ft (14,935m); ferry range 2,000nm (3,706km); combat radius (as fighter) 400nm (740km), (attack) 550nm (1,020km).
Payload: 1 20mm M61-A1 Vulcan multi-barrel cannon in upper fuselage; (fighter role) 2 AIM-9 Sidewinder, 4 AIM-7 Sparrow; (attack role) 2 AIM-9 Sidewinder, bombs and missiles for maximum total load of 17,000lb (7,710kg).
History: First flight Nov 1978; service delivery Feb 1981.
Users: US Navy, US Marine Corps.

The original requirement for the F/A-18 came as a result of the escalating costs of the F-14 Tomcat programme. In 1974 specifications for a new, smaller fighter designated VFAX were drawn up, and in 1975 the US Navy and the Marine Corps chose the F-18, developed by McDonnell Douglas and Northrop from the experimental YF-17. The need to reduce maintenance requirements aboard the carriers, the air groups of which were now to receive fixed-wing ASW squadrons in addition to their fighter and attack squadrons, resulted in the F-18 being given a dual interceptor/light attack role. This in turn brought an increase in weight and power over the original design. Costs have also rocketed, and the F/A-18 is now as expensive as the F-14 itself.

The Hornet has a very advanced array of cockpit displays which enables it to dispense with the second crewman — a feature which has attracted some criticism. Special attention has been given to increasing reliability. Conversion from fighter to attack configuration, and vice-versa, will be a simple operation involving only the replacement of pods and weapons; all aircraft have the

Above: An F/A-18 Hornet is launched from the port forward catapult of the carrier *Constellation* (CV 64). The F/A-18 will begin to replace the A-7 Corsair as the Navy's light attack aircraft from 1983. It has the advantage of easy conversion to fighter duties, thereby providing the USN carriers with a considerably increased flexibility.

same APG-65 radar and air/ground sensors. It was originally envisaged that the Hornet would replace the F-4 Phantom in six Navy and nine Marine fighter attack squadrons, the A-4 Skyhawk and AV-8A Harrier in seven Marine light attack squadrons, and the A-7 Corsair in 24 Navy light attack squadrons, but decisions to proceed with the AV-8B Harrier for the USMC and to continue F-14 Tomcat production for the Navy means that the F/A-18 will now replace only the Marine Phantoms and the Navy's Corsairs. The first aircraft were delivered to the Navy in February 1981, and carrier squadrons will begin to convert in 1983. More than 200 F/A-18s are on order for the Australian, Canadian and Spanish air forces.

Below: An F/A-18 Hornet in the fighter configuration, with two AIM-9L Sidewinder heat-seaking missiles on the wing-tips, and two AIM-7 Sparrow semi-active missiles visible beneath the fuselage. Note the low-contrast grey paint scheme.

McDonnell Douglas F-4 Phantom

Type: (Variants: see text) two-seat carrier-/land-based multi-role fighter.
Data: F-4S.
Dimensions: Length 58ft 3in (17·76m); span 38ft 5in (11·7m); height 16ft 3in (4·95m).
Weight: Empty 28,000lb (12,700kg); maximum (carrier) 58,000lb (26,308kg).
Engines: Two 17,900lb (8,120kg) thrust General Electric J79-10A single-shaft turbojets with afterburners.
Performance: Maximum speed 1,262kt (2,335km/h); service ceiling 60,000ft (18,288m); range 2,300nm (4,260km); combat radius (as fighter) 300nm (555km), (attack) 400nm (740km).
Payload: (Fighter role) 4 AIM-7 Sparrow and 4 AIM-9 Sidewinder AAMs; (attack role) centreline and 4 wing pylons for maximum total load of 16,000lb (7,257kg).
History: First flight May 1958; service delivery (F-4A) Feb 1960; first flight (F-4C) May 1963, (F-4E) June 1967.
Users: US Navy, US Marine Corps; UK (RAF).

Above: An RF-4B Phantom is recovered on the carrier *Midway* (CV 41) during CINCPAC exercise FLEETEX 83 off the Aleutians. The carriers *Enterprise* (CV 65) and *Coral Sea* (CV 43) were also involved in the exercise. F-4J/S Phantoms continue to operate from the older carriers of the Midway and Forrestal classes, but it is envisaged that those on the Forrestals will be replaced by F-14A Tomcats. Carrier-based Phantoms have also served with the Royal Navy (F-4K), prior to the decommissions of *Ark Royal* in 1978.

Left: A Marine F-4 Phantom belonging to VMFA-333 squadron lands aboard a carrier. The Marines operate twelve fighter attack squadrons at present but this figure will reduce to nine as the current F-4N/S models are replaced by the F/A-18 in the mid 1980s. All Marine squadrons are also served with the Royal Navy (F-4K), prior to the decommissioning been assigned to carriers for long deployments.

The F-4 Phantom began life as a gunless all-weather interceptor with advanced radar and a powerful battery of air-to-air missiles of both the semi-active (Sparrow) and infra-red (Sidewinder) homing types. The Phantom proved to be outstanding in all respects, and its considerable capacity for weapons delivery, which approached that of a specialised light attack aircraft, was exploited to full advantage during the Vietnam War. The Phantom came to be operated by the US Air Force and the Marines as a multi-purpose fighter, and the aircraft was purchased in large numbers by foreign air forces. The British Royal Navy operated 28 Phantoms (the F-4K with the Rolls-Royce Spey engine) from the carrier *Ark Royal* until the latter paid off in 1978, when her aircraft were reassigned to the RAF to operate from land bases.

Most of the aircraft in current service with the US Navy were originally F-4J models, of which 552 were built 1966-72; they have the improved AWG-10 doppler-pulse fire control radar and more powerful engines. A total of 265 of these aircraft have been updated to the F-4S configuration, which features a long-slatted airframe and a new jamming system (ALQ-162). Phantom F-4J/S models serve in eight Navy active squadrons, operating from older carriers of the Midway and Forrestal classes. Between 1972 and 1978 228 F-4Bs serving with the Navy and the Marines were upgraded to F-4N configuration. The F-4N serves with 12 Marine Corps Fighter Attack (VMFA) squadrons and with four reserve Navy squadrons. Twenty-one RF-4B aircraft serve with a single Marine Photo-Reconnaissance squadron. The Marine Corps Phantoms are being replaced by the F/A-18 Hornet, beginning in 1983-84.

USA
Sikorsky CH-53 Sea Stallion and Super Stallion

Type: (CH-53A/D) shipborne assault helicopter; (RH-53D) mine counter-measures helicopter; (CH-53E) shipborne heavy-lift replenishment helicopter (crew of 3 all versions).

Dimensions: Fuselage length (CH-53A/D) 67ft 2in (20·47m), (CH-53E) 73ft 4in (22·35m); main rotor diameter (CH-53A/D) 72ft 3in (22m), (CH-53E) 79ft (24·1m); height (CH-53A/D) 24ft 11in (7·6m), (CH-53E) 28ft 5in (8.66m).

Weight: Empty (CH-53A/D) 23,628lb (10,718kg), (CH-53E) 33,226lb (15,071kg); maximum (CH-53A/D) 42,000lb (19,051kg), (CH-53E) 73,500lb (33,339kg).

Engines: (CH-53A/D) two 3,925shp General Electric T64-413 turboshafts; (CH-53E) three 4,380shp General Electric T64-416 turboshafts.

Performance: Maximum speed 170kt (315km/h); service ceiling 21,000ft (6,400m); ferry range (CH-53A/D) 886nm (1,640km), (CH-53E) 1,120nm (2,075km).

Payload: (CH-53A/D) 38 troops or 8,000lb (3,630kg) cargo; (CH-53E) 32,200lb (14,605kg) cargo.

History: First flight Oct 1964; service delivery (CH-53A) May 1966, (CH-53D) March 1969, (RH-53) Sept 1973, (CH-53E) Dec 1980.

Users: (CH-53A/D) US Marine Corps; (RH-53) US Navy, Iran; (CH-53E) US Marine Corps, US Navy.

Right: The massive CH-53E Super Stallion, now entering service with the US Marine Corps. One of the world's most powerful heavy-lift helicopters, the CH-53E can lift 16 tons of cargo, and can recover any aircraft in the current US Navy or USMC inventory.Distinguishing points are the broad tail and third engine.

Right: RH-53 helicopters lift off from the carrier _Nimitz_ (CVN 68) for the ill-fated attempt to rescue US hostages held in Iran. The mission was abandoned when faults developed on a number of the helicopters taking part. In spite of this the RH-53 and its troop-carrying counterpart, the CH-53D Sea Stallion, are generally regarded as reliable machines. The CH-53D is the standard Marine heavy-lift helicopter, and is regularly deployed aboard amphibious assault ships. It can carry 38 fully-equipped troops or 8,000lb of cargo. The RH-53 is an MCM variant and currently equips three squadrons.

The CH-53 Sea Stallion is a heavy assault helicopter developed specifically for the US Marine Corps. It is a hybrid combining an enlarged Sea King fuselage and the six-bladed rotor and power train systems of the Army's CH-54 Skycrane helicopter. It can carry 38 fully-armed troops, with an alternative loading of two jeeps, two Hawk missiles or a 105mm howitzer, embarked via a rear-loading ramp. Delivery of the CH-53A began in 1966, with the improved CH-53D following in 1969. A total of 265 of both variants were built, and the Marine Corps operates seven helicopter squadrons each with 15-21 CH-53A/D, which provide LPH/LHA detachments.

The RH-53D mine countermeasures variant is operated by the US Navy. It is a basic CH-53A/D with upgraded engines (T64-GE-415), a strengthened fuselage, an automatic flight control system, and attachment points for a variety of MCM devices (Mk 103 mechanical, Mk 104 acoustic, Mk 105 magnetic, and Mk 106 magnetic/acoustic). The first Navy MCM squadron was equipped with 15 modified CH-53As, but 30 new-build RH-53Ds were delivered from September 1973, and three squadrons, each of 4-7 helicopters, are now operational. Six additional RH-53Ds were delivered to Iran.

The CH-53E Super Stallion is a three-engine heavy-lift derivative for Navy and USMC use. It can lift a massive 16 tons (50 per cent more than the CH-47 Chinook), a figure which accounts for 93 per cent of all heavy equipment in service with a Marine division. In the aircraft recovery role all current Navy and USMC types can be carried. A construction programme of 33 CH-53Es for the USMC, plus 16 for the Navy has been approved. An MH-53E MCM variant will eventually replace the RH-53D in the Navy's MCM squadrons.

USA
Sikorsky SH-3 Sea King

Type: (SH-3D/H) shipborne/land-based antisubmarine helicopter (crew of 4); (SH-3G) utility helicopter.
Data: SH-3D.
Dimensions: Fuselage length 54ft 9in (16·68m); main rotor diameter 62ft (18·9m); height 16ft 10in (5·13m).
Weight: Empty 11,865lb (5,382kg); maximum 20,500lb (9,299kg).
Engines: Two 1,400shp General Electric T58-10 turboshafts.
Performance: Maximum speed 144kt (267km/h); service ceiling 14,700ft (4,480m); range 625nm (1,160km); mission endurance 4½ hours.
Payload: 2 Mk 46 homing torpedoes.
History: First flight March 1959; service delivery (SH-3A) Sept 1961; (SH-3D) 1966.
Users: US Navy; Argentina, Belgium, Brazil, Canada, Iran, Italy (Agusta), Japan (Mitsubishi), Peru, Spain.

Right: An S-61B Sea King of the Japanese Maritime Self-Defense Force. 73 helicopters of this type were built under licence by Mitsubishi from the late 1960s onwards for the JMSDF, and 63 remain in service. Besides being operated from shore bases the Japanese Sea Kings serve aboard the four large helicopter destroyers of the Haruna and Shirane classes.

The SH-3 Sea King, which entered service more than 20 years ago, remains the standard carrier-based ASW helicopter in service with the US Navy. It is flown by the USAF and several foreign services in the transport and SAR role, and by other navies for ASW, and provided the basis for the similar Westland Sea King (see pages 82-85).

The earliest ASW model, the SH-3A, was operated from the antisubmarine carriers of the Essex class. A total of 255 were built for the US Navy, and the SH-3A served as the basis for 41 CH-124s (ex-CHSS-2) built under licence by United Aircraft of Canada, and 73 S-61Bs (ex-HSS-2) built under licence by Mitsubishi for the JMSDF. Twelve of the US Navy models were converted as SAR helicopters with armament and armour, and became HH-3As. A further 105 were converted as utility helicopters and became SH-3Gs. From 1966 the SH-3A was superseded in production by the SH-3D, of which 72 were built for the US Navy, 22 for Spain and four for Brazil. Four similar S-61Ds were purchased by Argentina, and Agusta of Italy built 24 under licence for the Italian Navy, and seven for Iran; a follow-up order of 30 for the Italian Navy was placed in the late 1970s. The current SH-3H variant in service with the US Navy is a multi-purpose version of the SH-3G, with new ASW equipment. All remaining SH-3A and SH-3D models are to be converted to "H" standard.

The US Navy currently operates 11 carrier-based ASW helicopter squadrons, each with six SH-3D/H, plus two readiness squadrons. SH-3Gs serve in the four helicopter combat support squadrons. The Sea King is now approaching the end of its service life, but as yet no replacement has been sanctioned; a modified version of the SH-60B Seahawk with dipping sonar (the SH-60F) is one proposal under consideration.

Above: Three-view of the uprated SH-3H Sea King.

Below: An Agusta-built SH-3D of the Italian Navy. The Italian SH-3Ds operate from shore bases.

Sikorsky SH-60B Seahawk

Type: (SH-60B) shipborne antisubmarine helicopter (crew of 3).
Dimensions: Fuselage length 50ft (15·24m); main rotor diameter 53ft 8in (16·36m); height 17ft 2in (5·23m).
Weight: Empty 13,648lb (6,191kg); maximum 21,884lb (9,926kg).
Engines: Two 1,690shp General Electric T700-401 turboshafts.
Performance: Maximum speed 126kt (234km/h); service ceiling 18.500ft (5,639m); mission endurance 3½ hours.
Payload: 2 Mk 46 homing torpedoes.
History: First flight Dec 1979; service delivery 1984.
Users: US Navy.

The SH-60B Seahawk is being developed as the basis of the LAMPS III ASW system for operation from cruisers, destroyers and frigates of the US Navy. After first considering a light purpose-built ASW helicopter similar in size and capability to the types in service with the West European navies (LAMPS II), the US Navy opted instead for a variant of the Army's UH-60A (UTTAS) troop-carrying helicopter, which had the advantage of a much heavier payload

and a greater mission endurance. The SH-60B has a different landing gear from the Army model, and folding systems for the main rotor and tail. The helicopter features an advanced rotor design and an engine built from individual modules which can be replaced using nine common tools. A RAST (Recovery Assist, Secure and Traverse) haul-down and handling system is also under development to enable the Seahawk to take off and land in sea conditions up to Sea State 5. The first 18 SH-60Bs out of a projected total of 204 were ordered in April 1982. Deliveries began in 1983.

Like its predecessor, LAMPS I, the LAMPS III system is essentially ship-based in that overall control remains with the surface ship, which also processes data from the helicopter's own sensors. Seahawk operations are monitored by an acoustic sensor operator (ASO) in the ship's sonar room, a remote radar operator (REMRO) and an electronic warfare operator (EWO) in the ship's CIC, and an air tactical control officer (ATACO) who co-ordinates the activities of the three operators and who is in effect the tactical mission commander. Aboard the helicopter there is a crew of three: a pilot, an airborne tactical officer (ATO), who monitors the ship's tactical direction of the mission, and a sensor operator. In addition to its primary antisubmarine mission the Seahawk also provides over-the-horizon targeting for a ship's Harpoon anti-ship missiles, and anti-missile defence.

Left: An SH-60B Seahawk antisubmarine helicopter conducts sea trials from the frigate *McInerny* (FFG 8). The frigates of this class are designed to operate two SH-60Bs, for which they are provided with a large double hangar and a RAST handling system. The SH-60B can also provide OTH guidance for anti-ship missiles.

Below: An SH-60B of HSL-34 parked on the flight deck of the Spruance-class destroyer *Arthur W. Radford*. The SH-60B will operate from all US Navy surface vessels completed since the mid-1970s, and an "F" variant may replace the Sea King on the Navy's carriers.

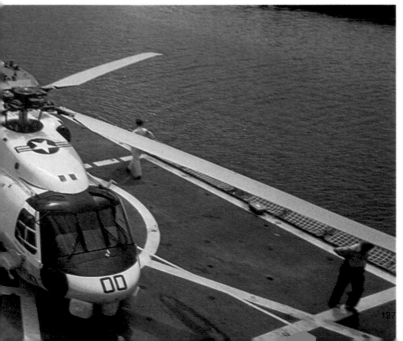

Vought A-7 Corsair II

Type: (Variants: see text) single seat carrier-/land-based light attack aircraft.
Data: A-7E.
Dimensions: Length 46ft 1½in (14·06m); span 38ft 9in (11·8m); height 16ft 1in (4·9m).
Weight: Empty 19,781lb (8,972kg); maximum 42,000lb (19,050kg).
Engines: One 15,000lb (6,804kg) thrust Allison TF-41-2 (Spey derivative) turbofan.
Performance: Maximum speed 600kt (1,112km/h) at sea level; service ceiling 42,600ft (12,985m); range 2,485nm (4,604km); combat radius 700nm (1,296km).
Payload: 1 20mm M61-A1 Vulcan multi-barrel cannon on left side fuselage; 6 wing and 2 fuselage stores pylons for maximum total load of 15,000lb (6,804kg).
History: First flight Sept 1965; service delivery (A-7A) Oct 1966; (A-7E) July 1969.
Users: US Navy.

The A-7 Corsair was developed as a replacement for the A-4 Skyhawk in the day attack role. A simple, robust, lightweight aircraft with minimal avionics was specified. Vought proposed an adaptation of the successful F-8 Crusader

Right: An A-7A Corsair II of VA-195 "Dam Busters" belonging to the carrier *Kitty Hawk* (CV 63). All US carriers have two light attack squadrons each comprising twelve Corsairs, totalling 288 front-line machines.

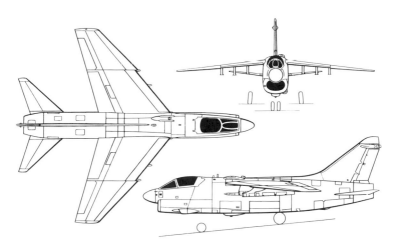

Above: Three-view of the A-7D Corsair; A-7E is similar.

interceptor, and the adoption of this proposal helped to speed development and delivery. By restricting performance to high subsonic — the F-8 Crusader was capable of Mach 1·7 — structure weight was reduced, range dramatically increased and weapon load quadrupled. One hundred and ninety-nine A-7As were built, closely followed by 196 A-7Bs. Later models incorporated the customary improvements in avionics to provide a limited all-weather and night capability. In 1966 the Corsair was adopted by the US Air Force, resulting in an improved A-7D model with the more powerful T41 engine, a multi-barrel M61 Vulcan 20mm cannon, and all-weather avionics. The US Navy subsequently adopted the same model with an uprated T41 engine, and 596 A-7Es were delivered. Plans for an RF-7E photo-reconnaissance aircraft for the carrier air wings were abandoned in favour of the RF-4A Phantom. Sixty A-7H Corsairs derived from the Air Force version have been sold to Greece.

There are 24 US Navy carrier-based squadrons (two per air wing) each of 12 A-7Es, plus four reserve squadrons with older A-7 aircraft. From the mid-1900s the Corsair will be phased out in favour of the F/A-18 Hornet. In 1981-83 the Navy bought 91 FLIR (Forward-Looking Infra-Red) pods and 231 FLIR installations, the latter including new Marconi HUDs for improved night capability.

Left: An A-7E Corsair II of VA-86 "Sidewinders" lands aboard *Nimitz* (CVN 68) during NATO exercise TEAMWORK 80 off Northern Norway. The Corsair has proved to be a sturdy, reliable aircraft, but has been in service since 1966, and is soon to be replaced by the dual-role F/A-18 Hornet.

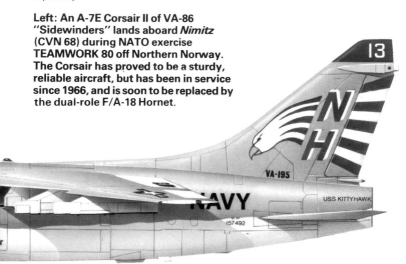

USA

Vought F-8 Crusader

Type: (F-8E (FN)) single-seat carrier-based interceptor.
Data: F-8E(FN).
Dimensions: Length 54ft 6in (16·6m); span 35ft 8in (10·87m); height 15ft 9in (4·8m).
Weight: Empty 19,751lb (8,960kg); maximum loaded 34,000lb (15,420kg).
Engines: One 18,000lb (8,165kg) thrust Pratt & Whitney J57-20A two-shaft turbojet with afterburner.
Performance: Maximum speed 868kt (1,609km/h) at altitude; service ceiling 50,000ft (15,240m); range 1,500nm (2,780km); combat radius 370nm (686km).
Payload: 4 20mm Colt Mk 12 cannon; 4 AIM-9 Sidewinder or 2 Matra R.530 AAMs.
History: First flight March 1955; service delivery (F-8U) March 1957; (F-8E(FN)) 1966.
Users: France.

The F-8 Crusader began life as a carrier-based day fighter with the US Navy. It was the first production aircraft capable of speeds in excess of 1,000mph, and proved extremely manoeuvrable. A total of 1,261 Crusaders were built, and of

Right: Two F-8E (FN) Crusaders of the Marine Nationale. 42 were purchased from the USA in the 1960s to operate as carrier-based interceptors.

Below: An F-8E Crusader is lined up on the waist catapult of the carrier *Clemenceau*. Only 15 aircraft remain in front-line service, and these will be phased out in the mid-1980s. Note the variable incidence wing, the travel of which was reduced for the French Navy aircraft in order to assist carrier landing.

these 446 were rebuilt in 1966-71 when improvements were made in all-weather capability and weapons delivery systems. The aircraft remained in service as an interceptor aboard the smaller US attack carriers well into the 1970s. High speed made the Crusader well-suited to the reconnaissance role, and an RF-8A photo-reconnaissance model was introduced in the early stages of the aircraft's development. Three-plane detachments of rebuilt RF-8Gs remained in service aboard the big super-carriers into the early 1980s, the last squadron (VFP-63) being disbanded only in June 1982.

The small size of the Crusader made it the only suitable high-performance jet fighter available when the French light fleet carriers *Clemenceau* and *Foch* were completed in the early 1960s. With the failure of French carrier-based interceptor projects, 42 F-8Es were purchased in 1963 for delivery in 1966. A number of special modifications were necessary to enable the Crusader to operate from the French carriers. These included the replacement of the original fire control radar by one compatible with the French Matra R.530 air-to-air missile, and a number of modifications to the airframe (double aileron and flap deflection, enlarged tail surfaces, and a 2-degree reduction in the travel of the variable-incidence wing) aimed at reducing the Crusader's landing speed by some 15kt (28km/h). Fifteen F-8Es remain in service with 12F, which provides an interceptor squadron of 10 aircraft to either of the two carriers, but the Aéronavale intends to phase out its Crusaders in the mid-1980s and to replace them with Super Etendard strike fighters armed with AAMs.

Land-based Aviation

FRANCE
Dassault Breguet Atlantic

Type: (Br.1150, Br.1160(ATL)) long-range maritime patrol aircraft (crew of 12).
Data: Br.1160.
Dimensions: Length 107ft 0¼in (32·62m); span 122ft 4½in (37·3m); height 37ft 3in (11·35m).
Weight: Empty 55,775lb (25,300kg); maximum 101,850lb (46,200kg).
Engines: Two 6,220ehp Rolls-Royce Tyne 21 two-shaft turboprops.
Performance: Maximum speed 355kt (658km/h) at altitude; patrol speed 170kt (315km/h); service ceiling 30,000ft (9,150m); patrol endurance 18 hours; ferry range 4,400nm (8,150km).
Payload: Weapons bay for eight homing torpedoes or two AM.39 air-to-surface missiles, depth charges and bombs; four underwing racks for up to 7,716lb (3,500kg) of stores including rockets, air-to-surface missiles or containers.
History: First flight (Br.1150) Oct 1961; service delivery Dec 1966; first flight (Br.1160) May 1981.
Users: France; FRG, Italy, Netherlands, Pakistan.

In 1959 the Breguet Atlantic (Br.1150) was the winning contender in a competition to find a standard NATO LRMP aircraft. As with most such competitions, the result did not inhibit the development of other national designs, but an Atlantic programme was launched by France and Germany, which ordered 40 and 20 respectively; further orders followed from the Netherlands (nine aircraft) and Italy (18). The airframes were built in all four countries, the engines produced by a European consortium, and Britain and the USA supplied much of the avionics. A "double bubble" fuselage was adopted to provide adequate space for the weapon/sensor payload beneath the main tactical compartment. Five of the German Atlantics are specially fitted for the ELINT mission.

The aircraft covered in this section are operated exclusively from shore bases. They are basically of two types: large land-based bombers used for maritime strike; and long-range maritime patrol aircraft with ASW or reconnaissance missions.

The Atlantic has proved efficient and reliable in service, and in the late 1970s the French decided to re-open the Breguet production line to build an improved model, the ATL2. This aircraft, designated Br. 1160, is based on the airframe and powerplant of the original Atlantic, but has a completely new outfit of weapons, sensors and displays. An all-digital tactical control system will be provided, and the ATL2 can carry up to four AM.39 Exocet anti-ship missiles on underwing pylons. Forty-two aircraft are planned, with delivery from 1985 onwards; they will replace not only the current active Br.1150s but also the 12 remaining P-2 Neptunes. Fourteen of the German Atlantics remaining in service are having their electronics updated, the prime contractor being Dornier.

Above: An Atlantic Br. 1150 of the French Aéronavale with ventral radome extended.

Below: The Atlantic "Nouvelle Generation" (ANG) will replace the older Atlantics and Neptunes of the Aéronavale.

Panavia Tornado

Type: (Tornado IDS) two-seat multi-role strike aircraft; (Tornado ADV) two-seat air defence aircraft.

Dimensions: Length (IDS) 54ft 9½in (16·7m), (ADV) 59ft 3in (18·06m); span (25°) 45ft 7¼in (13·9m), (65°) 28ft 2½in (8·6m); height 18ft 8½in (5·7m).

Weight: Empty 24,000lb (10,890kg); maximum 60,000lb (18,150kg).

Engines: Two 16,000lb (7,258kg) thrust Turbo Union RB199 Mk 101 three-shaft augmented turbofans.

Performance: Maximum speed 1,152kt (2,135km/h) at altitude; 791kt (1,465km/h) at sea level; service ceiling over 50,000ft (15,240m); range (internal fuel) 870nm (1,610km).

Payload: (IDS) 2 27mm Mauser cannon in forward fuselage; 4 tandem and 4 underwing pylons for bombs, Sea Eagle/Kormoran ASMs or drop tanks, maximum total load 18,000lb (8,165kg); (ADV) 1 27mm Mauser cannon; 4 Sky Flash and 2 AIM-9 Sidewinder AAMs.

History: First flight (prototype) Aug 1974; (production IDS) July 1979; (production ADV) Sept 1979.

Users: FGR (Marineflieger), Italy, UK (RAF).

The Tornado is derived from a requirement for a Multi-Role Combat Aircraft (MRCA) able to undertake a variety of strike missions within the European Theatre. Developed by a consortium in which the British (BAe) and Germans (MBB) hold a majority share, with Aeritalia accounting for the remaining 15 per cent, the Tornado is a sophisticated variable geometry aircraft employing fly-by-wire technology, and fitted with advanced avionics and fire control systems. The variety of external stores which can be carried exceeds that of any other aircraft.

A total of 385 aircraft (of which some 220 will be of the Tornado IDS strike version) is projected for the RAF, 202 for the Luftwaffe plus 112 for the Marineflieger, and a further 100 for the Regia Aeronautica. The Tornados serving with the Marineflieger replace the F-104G Starfighters which previously made up the two German maritime strike squadrons (MFG 1 and 2, based at Schleswig and Eggebek respectively). They normally carry four (max 8) Kormoran missiles in the anti-shipping role; Kormoran has a range of 20nm (37km) and has a 353lb (160kg) warhead. A number of the RAF Tornados are also being allocated to the maritime strike mission, armed with the Sea Eagle ASM; they are replacing the Buccaneer S.2s currently employed in this role. A British air defence variant, the Tornado F.2, will be tasked with the interception of Soviet long-range maritime bombers attempting to strike at naval installations in the UK and at warships operating in the East Atlantic area — a role perfomed at present by Phantom FGR.2s.

Right: A Tornado maritime strike aircraft of the German Marineflieger. These aircraft will be armed with four Kormoran anti-ship missiles.

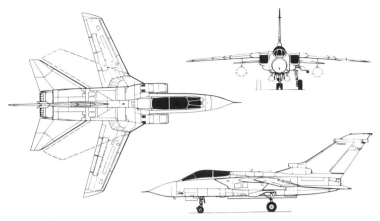

Above: Three-view of the Tornado IDS.

Below: A prototype F.2 air defence version for the RAF.

Left: A Tornado multi-role strike aircraft of the Luftwaffe. 202 will be built for the Air Force, plus 112 for the Marineflieger.

Kawasaki P-2J

Type: (P-2J) land-based LRMP aircraft.
Dimensions: Length 95ft 10¾ (29·32m); span 101ft 3½in (30·87m); height 29ft 3½in (8·93m).
Weight: Empty 42,500lb (19,277kg); maximum 75,000lb (34,019kg).
Engines: Two 2,850hp General Electric T64-10 single-shaft turboprops; two 3,085lb (1,400kg) thrust Ishikawajima-Harima J3-7C turbojets.
Performance: Maximum speed (jets) 350kt (649km/h); typical cruising speed 217kt (402km/h); service ceiling 30,000ft (9,144m); range 2,400nm (4,445km).
Payload: Mk 44/46 homing torpedoes, depth bombs, rockets; maximum internal load 8,000lb (3,630kg).
History: First flight July 1966; service delivery Oct 1969.
Users: Japan (JMSDF).

Right: A Kawasaki P-2J of the Japanese Maritime Self-Defense Force. These long-range ASW patrol aircraft are now obsolescent, and the 80 remaining in service will be replaced by a slightly larger force of P-3C Orions during the 1980s.

Shin Meiwa PS-1

Type: (PS-1) antisubmarine flying boat (crew of 9); (US-1) search and rescue amphibian (crew of 9).
Data: PS-1.
Dimensions: Fuselage length 109ft 11in (33·5m); span 108ft 8¾in (33·14m); height 31ft 10½in (9·7m).
Weight: Empty 58,000lb (26,300kg); maximum 94,800lb (43,000kg).
Engines: Four 3,060ehp Ishikawajima-built General Electric T64-IHI-10 single-shaft turboprops.
Performance: Maximum speed 295kt (547km/h); service ceiling 29,500ft (9,000m); range (loaded) 1,170nm (2,167km).
Payload: 4 depth bombs in internal weapons bay; 4 Mk 44/46 homing torpedoes in containers on underwing pylons; launchers on wing tips for triple groups of 5in rockets.
History: First flight (prototype) Oct 1967; (PS-1) 1972; service delivery 1975.
Users: Japan (JMSDF).

Forty-eight Lockheed P-2H Neptunes were built under licence by Kawasaki for the JMSDF 1959-66, and a modified P-2J variant was subsequently developed and built as a successor. A longer fuselage was adopted together with a broader tail, new turboprops and booster turbojets were installed, and fuel capacity was increased. The electronics suite, which features Jezebel/Julie sonobuoys and their associated monitoring equipment, is now somewhat dated, and the 80 P-2Js currently in service with the JMSDF are being replaced by Kawasaki-built P-3C Orions over the next few years.

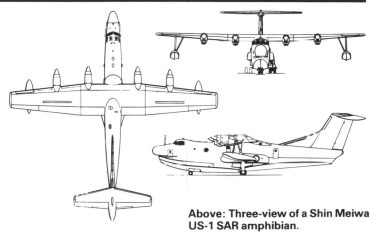

Above: Three-view of a Shin Meiwa US-1 SAR amphibian.

Similar in conception to, but somewhat larger than the Soviet Beriev Be-12, the PS-1 is the world's only other modern military flying boat. It entered service with the JMSDF in 1975, the PX-S prototype having demonstrated the feasibility of nuclear submarine hunting operations using such an aircraft. The PS-1 has the advantage of being able to alight on the surface during the search and localisation phase and to listen with its large sonar, thereby obviating the need to expend large numbers of sonobuoys. The surface search radar is located in a projecting nose radome, as in its Soviet counterpart. Nineteen PS-1s are currently in service. The JMSDF later received eight US-1 amphibians tasked in the SAR role. Both types have a separate T58 engine to provide boundary-layer control blowing over the wings and tail to enable them to fly very slowly under full control, and take off and land in shorter distances.

Left: A Shin Meiwa US-1 amphibian. The US-1 is a search and rescue (SAR) version; eight were built in the late 1970s. Its ASW counterpart is the PS-1, of which 19 are currently in service. Only the Japanese and the Soviets have persisted with the amphibian, which is however particularly well-suited to the medium-range antisubmarine role: unlike landplanes, it can "sprint and drift".

BAe (HSA) Buccaneer

Type: (S.2) two-seat land-based attack and reconnaissance.
Dimensions: Length 63ft 5in (19·33m); span 44ft (13·41m); height 16ft 3in (4·95m).
Weight: Empty 30,000lb (13,610kg); maximum 62,000lb (28,123kg).
Engines: Two 11,030lb (5,003kg) thrust Rolls-Royce Spey 101 two-shaft turbofans.
Performance: Maximum speed 560kt (1,038km/h) at sea level; service ceiling over 40,000ft (12,192m); range (with weapon load) 2,000nm (3,700km).
Payload: 4 1,000lb (454kg) bombs in internal rotating bomb bay; 4 wing pylons each rated at 3,000lb (1,361kg); maximum total load (internal and external) 16,000lb (7,257kg).
History: First flight (prototype) April 1958; (production S.1) Jan 1962; (prototype S.2) May 1963; (production S.2) June 1964.
Users: UK (RAF).

Designed at the outset as a carrier-based low-level all-weather medium attack aircraft, the Buccaneer was virtually the only aircraft project to survive the notorious Defence White Paper of 1957. The carrier *Ark Royal* embarked the first operational squadron in 1962, and the other British first-line carriers soon followed. The S.2 variant which is currently in service was originally intended to operate from the carrier CVA-01; it has more powerful engines and an improved radar/navigation/attack system. The first 84 aircraft were ordered for the Royal Navy but, following the cancellation of CVA-01, most were transferred to RAF Strike Command, which ordered a further 43 aircraft in 1968. A South African order for 16 aircraft was placed in 1963. Ten S.2D Buccaneers, plus four S.2C tanker aircraft, continued to operate as 809 naval air squadron aboard the carrier *Ark Royal* until the latter decommissioned in late 1978, when they too transferred to RAF Strike Command. As 208 squadron they are one of two squadrons (the other is 12 squadron) based at airfields in the UK and allocated to maritime strike duties.

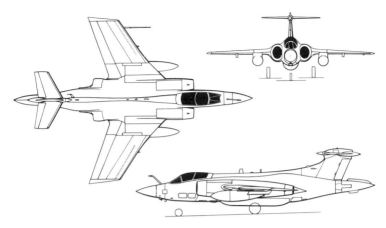

Above: Three-view of Buccaneer S.2 with bomb-door fuel tank.

The Buccaneer was one of the largest aircraft to operate from British carriers, and the ex-Navy aircraft have not only folding wings, but a folding nose and tail-cone which reduce overall length to 50ft 7in (15·4m). The internal payload, which can include a nuclear weapon or a six-camera reconnaissance package, is carried in a revolving bomb bay. The basic RAF Buccaneer was the S.2A; the basic Navy variant the S.2C. The S.2B (RAF) and S.2D (RN) variants have the internal avionics needed by Martel anti-radiation (AS.37) or TV-guided anti-ship (AJ.168) missiles. It is envisaged that the Buccaneer will be replaced by the Tornado IDS during the 1980s.

Below: Although its avionics are now somewhat dated, the Buccaneer remains a formidable aircraft in the low-level strike role. A heavy payload can be carried in a revolving bomb bay and on four wing pylons. RAF Buccaneers are scheduled to receive "fire-and-forget" Sea Eagle ASMs.

BAe (HSA) Nimrod

Type: (MR.1 and 2) long-range maritime patrol aircraft (crew of 12); (R.1.) ELINT aircraft; (AEW.3) airborne early warning aircraft.
Data: MR.2
Dimensions: Length 126ft 9in (38·63m); span 114ft 10in (35m); height 29ft 8½in (9·1m).
Weight: Empty 92,000lb (41,730kg); maximum 192,000lb (87,090kg).
Engines: Four 12,140lb (5,507kg) thrust Rolls-Royce Spey 250 two-shaft turbofans.
Performance: Maximum speed 500kt (926km/h); patrol speed 425kt (787km/h); service ceiling 42,000ft (12,800m); range 5,000nm (9,260km); patrol endurance 12 hours.
Payload: Internal weapons bay for up to 6 Mk 46/Stingray homing torpedoes, depth bombs, sonobuoys; 2 wing pylons for Martel or AS.12 ASMs (some MR.2s fitted for AIM-9 Sidewinder AAMs).
History: First flight (prototype) May 1967; service delivery (MR.1) Oct 1969; (MR.2) Aug 1979.
Users: UK (RAF).

The Nimrod is the only LRMP aircraft in the world to employ jet propulsion, the other types in service all being turboprop aircraft. Jet propulsion gives the Nimrod a high transit speed, resulting in an ability to react quickly to a

Right: A Nimrod AEW.3 of the RAF. The distinctive nose and tail radomes each give 180° coverage. The Marconi search radar is optimised for use over water, and the eleven aircraft under conversion will provide coverage of the entire North Atlantic area against surprise enemy attack.

submarine datum established by broad-area detection systems such as SOSUS, or passive arrays towed by surface ships.

Forty-three of a total of 49 aircraft built were completed to the MR.1 (ASW) configuration. Three Nimrods were completed as electronic intelligence (ELINT) aircraft, and designated R.1, and the final three MR.1s were diverted as trials aircraft for the Nimrod AEW.3 airborne early warning variant.

The original Nimrod MR.1 proved to be reliable, but its effectiveness in the antisubmarine role was inhibited by its relatively austere electronics outfit. This defect is now being remedied by a major modernisation programme involving the installation of an EMI Searchwater radar, a Marconi AQS-901 acoustic processing and display system matched with the Barra sonobuoy, and a new Central Tactical Data System based on a Marconi 920 ATC digital computer. Thirty-four MR.1s are being converted to the MR.2 configuration; they serve with three operational LRMP squadrons at Kinloss (120, 201, 206) and one at St. Mawgan (42). Eleven additional MR.1s are being converted to the airborne early warning configuration and will replace the elderly Shackleton in the maritime reconnaissance role. The AEW.3 conversion involves the fitting of large radomes in the nose and tail of the Nimrod for 360-degree coverage.

Below: A Nimrod MR.2 LRMP aircraft in the new mid-grey low-contrast paint scheme. During the Falklands conflict a number of aircraft were fitted with fuel probes to enable them to operate over the South Atlantic from Ascension Island.

Beriev Be-12 (M-12) Mail

Type: (Be-12) multi-role reconnaissance amphibian (crew of 4-9).
Dimensions: Length 99ft (30·17m); span 97ft 5¾in (29·71m); height 22ft 11½in (7m).
Weight: Empty 44,092lb (20,000kg); maximum 64,925lb (29,450kg).
Engines: Two 4,190ehp Ivchenko AI-20D single-shaft turboprops.
Performance: Maximum speed 329kt (610km/h); service ceiling 37,000ft (11,280m); range 2,160nm (4,000km); operational radius 702nm (1,300km).
Payload: Internal weapons bay for variety of ASW weapons; 2-4 underwing hardpoints for homing torpedoes or other stores.
History: First flight 1960; service delivery 1965.
Users: USSR (AV-MF).

This versatile amphibian has been the standard medium-range Soviet anti-submarine aircraft since the early 1960s. A search radar is mounted in a projecting nose radome, and a MAD stinger extends some 15ft beyond the tail. Depth bombs and sonobuoys are carried in an internal weapons bay abaft the wing, and there are underwing hardpoints for additional stores and weapons. Some 80 Be-12s remain in service with the Soviet AV-MF, most being deployed to the Northern and Black Sea Fleet areas.

Right: A Be-12 Mail antisubmarine amphibian takes off on a patrol. The Be-12 has been in service since the mid-1960s and serves predominantly in the Black Sea and Northern Fleet areas. Note the projecting nose radome for the search radar.

Mil Mi-14 Haze

Type: (Mi-14) land-based antisubmarine helicopter (crew of 4-5?).
Dimensions: Fuselage length 60ft (18·3m); main rotor diameter 69ft 10½in (21·3m); height 15ft 7½in (4·8m).
Weight: Empty 17,650lb (8,000kg); maximum 26,460lb (12,000kg).
Engines: Two 2,200shp Isotov TV3-117A free-turbine turboshafts.
Performance: Maximum speed 140kt (260km/h); service ceiling 14,765ft (4,500m); range 270nm (500km); mission endurance 2½ hours.
Payload: Homing torpedoes, depth bombs; possibly ASMs.
History: First flight (V-14) 1973; service delivery (Mi-14) by 1977.
Users: USSR (AV-MF); Bulgaria, Indonesia.

Derived from the Mi-8 Hip transport helicopter, the Mi-14 is a large land-based antisubmarine helicopter, rather larger, heavier and more powerful than the Western Sea King. It has a boat-shaped lower fuselage with stabilising sponsons into which the main landing gear retracts. There is a large chin search radar, and a towed MAD "bird" is stowed beneath the forward end of the tailboom in the manner of the earlier Mi-4 Hound (now being withdrawn from service). The absence of visible external attachments suggests that there is an internal weapons bay. Besides an estimated 100 Mi-14s currently in service, a number of Mi-8 Hip helicopters have been fitted for aerial minesweeping. Two such helicopters operated from the ASW cruiser *Leningrad* during the Suez Canal clearance operations in 1974.

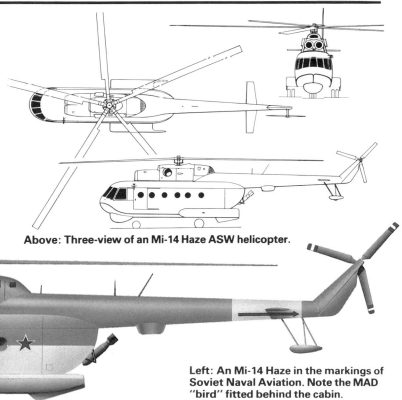

Above: Three-view of an Mi-14 Haze ASW helicopter.

Left: An Mi-14 Haze in the markings of Soviet Naval Aviation. Note the MAD "bird" fitted behind the cabin.

Ilyushin Il-38 May

Type: (Il-38) long-range maritime patrol aircraft (crew of 8-12).
Dimensions: Length 129ft 10in (39·6m); span 122ft 8½in (37·4m); height 35ft (10·7m).
Weight: Empty 80,470lb (36,500kg); maximum 143,300lb (65,000kg).
Engines: Four 4,250ehp Ivchenko AI-20M single-shaft turboprops.
Performance: Maximum speed 380kt (704km/h) at altitude; patrol speed 174kt (322km/h); range 3,900nm (7,223km); patrol endurance 12 hours.
Payload: Weapons bay for homing torpedoes, depth bombs, sonobuoys; maximum total load 15,432lb (7,000kg).
History: Service delivery 1969.
Users: USSR (AV-MF); India.

Like the US P-3 Orion, the Il-38 May was developed from a turboprop passenger transport (the Il-18 Coot). It is a new purpose-built variant designed to incorporate the necessary sensors and weapons for ASW search and strike. Modifications to the basic Il-18 design include moving the wing forward, to counter a shift in the aircraft's centre of gravity caused by the location of the weapons bay and a prominent search radar beneath the forward fuselage. The rear fuselage contains only sensors (including a MAD stinger in the tail) and sonobuoy launchers. No deep lower lobe has been added to the fuselage, which has the same cross-section as that of the civil transport. The weapons bay, and consequently the payload, is therefore small by Western standards; no exterior stores pylons have been observed. The electronics outfit is also relatively austere, with few visible protrusions for aerials.

Some 70 aircraft of this type are thought to be in service with the AV-MF. A

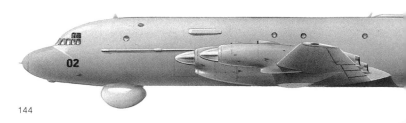

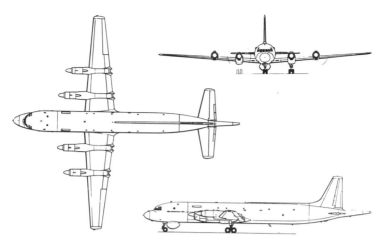

Above: Three-view of an Il-38 May ASW patrol aircraft.

number operated from Egyptian bases in the early 1970s in support of Soviet antisubmarine operations in the Eastern Mediterranean. However, the most likely mission of the May in the event of hostilities between NATO and the Warsaw Pact is in support of the Soviet Navy's own ballistic missile submarines (SSBNs) in the Northern and Pacific Fleet areas. Rebuilt Il-18s serve in the ELINT role.

Left: An Il-38 May ASW patrol aircraft of the AV-MF is escorted away from the US carrier *Midway* (CV 41) in the Indian Ocean by an F-4J Phantom of VF-161. The May is an exceptionally "clean" aircraft, with few visible aerials or other protrusions.

Below: An Il-38 of the Indian Navy. India has been the only export customer for the Il-38. Three serve with INAS 315 at Dabolim. The major weakness of the aircraft lies in its limited payload.

Tupolev Tu-16 Badger

Type: (Badger A) tanker aircraft; (Badger C,G) land-based strike bomber; (Badger D,E) reconnaissance bomber; (Badger F) ELINT aircraft; (Badger H) stand-off or escort ECM aircraft; (Badger J) ECM/EW aircraft; (Badger K) electronic reconnaissance aircraft; (crew of 6 in most versions).
Dimensions: Length 114ft 2in (34·8m); (Badger D) 120ft 9in (36·8m); span 109ft 11in (33·5m); height 35ft 5in (10·8m).
Weight: Empty 92,590lb (42,000kg); maximum 169,755lb (77,000kg).
Engines: Two 20,945lb (9,500kg) thrust Mikulin RD-3M turbojets.
Performance: Maximum speed 510kt (945km/h) at altitude; cruise speed 420kt (780km/h); service ceiling 42,650ft (13,000m); range (with missile load) 2,600nm (4,815km).
Payload: 6-8 23mm cannon; (Badger C,G) 2 AS-4 Kitchen, AS-5 Kelt or AS-6 Kingfish ASMs on underwing pylons.
History: First flight 1952; service delivery (Badger A) 1955; (Badger C) 1961; (Badger D) 1965.
Users: USSR (AV-MF).

Tu-16 Badger bombers still make up the bulk of the anti-shipping strike force of the Soviet naval air arm, the AV-MF. The Badger began life in Air Force service as a strategic bomber, but some 400 were transferred to the AV-MF from the early 1960s for employment in the surface strike and maritime reconnaissance roles. Some 250 Badgers are thought to remain in service as strike aircraft. Most are Badger Gs, armed from the outset with two AS-5 Kelt missiles on underwing pylons, but now being converted to carry the AS-6 Kingfish; the remainder are of the older Badger C variant, which initially carried a single AS-2 Kipper missile beneath its fuselage but now also carries the AS-6

Below: A Tu-16 Badger F, photographed by an RAF Nimrod over the North Atlantic. The Badger F is employed for electronic intelligence, and can be distinguished from other variants by the two small electronic pods carried on pylons beneath the wings. Tu-16s engaged in ESM frequently work in pairs.

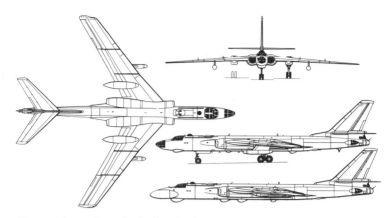

Above: Three-view of a Badger F with side view of Badger D.

Kingfish on wing pylons. Soviet anti-ship missiles are much larger than their Western counterparts, being designed for launch at long range against a heavily-defended carrier task force. The range of the AS-6 Kingfish is estimated at 135-302nm (250-560km). The Badger Cs and Gs are shared fairly evenly between the four Soviet fleet areas, and are backed up by a force of some 70 Badger A tanker aircraft. They are now being steadily replaced by the Tu-26 Backfire B, although it remains to be seen whether replacement can be on a one-for-one basis.

The remaining 70 Badger aircraft in service with the AV-MF are maritime reconnaissance and EW models. The Badger D has an enlarged chin radar and three ventral aerial fairings, and may have a missile guidance function in addition to the maritime surveillance role. The Badger E is a photo reconnaissance variant, with a glazed nose and camera pallets in the bomb bay; the Badger F is an FLINT variant, carrying receiver pods on its underwing pylons; and the Badger J has a high-power jamming system in a large ventral radome.

Tupolev Tu-20 Bear

Type: (Bear C) maritime reconnaissance aircraft; (Bear D) maritime reconnaissance/missile guidance; (Bear F) long-range ASW patrol aircraft (crew of 7-12).

Dimensions: Length (Bear C/D) 155ft 10in (47·5m), (Bear F) 162ft 5in (49·5m); span 167ft 8in (51·1m); height 39ft 9in (12·12m).

Weight: Empty (Bear C/D) 165,344lb (75,000kg), (Bear F) 178,571lb (81,000kg); maximum (Bear C/D) 374,780lb (170,000kg), (Bear F) 414,462lb (188,000kg).

Engines: Four 14,795ehp Kuznetsov NK-12M turboprops.

Performance: Maximum speed 456kt (845km/h) at altitude; cruise speed 378kt (700km/h); service ceiling 44,300ft (13,500m); range 6,775nm (12,550km); patrol endurance (Bear F) 28 hours.

Payload: 6 23mm cannon in three remotely-controlled barbettes; (Bear F) homing torpedoes, depth bombs, sonobuoys in internal bomb-bay.

History: First flight 1954; service delivery (Bear A) 1956; (Bear C) 1964; (Bear D) 1967; (Bear F) 1973.

Users: USSR (AV-MF).

Above: A Tu-20 Bear D of the Soviet naval air arm, the AV-MF. These aircraft are frequently seen over the North Atlantic. They are a key element in the Soviet Ocean Surveillance System (SOSS), for which role they are fitted with a wide variety of antennae, and they can in addition provide mid-course guidance for ship-launched cruise missiles such as the SS-N-3 Shaddock and the SS-N-12.

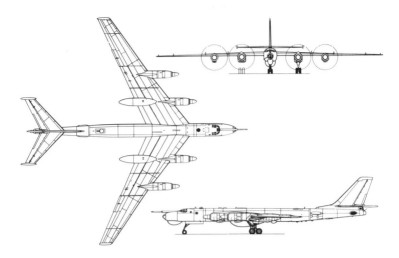

Above: Three-view of a Tu-20 Bear D.

The Tu-20 (bureau designation Tu-95) Bear was developed to meet Soviet Air Force requirements for a strategic bomber with intercontinental range and a heavy load of free-fall bombs. More than 100 of the Bear A and Bear B variants — the latter equipped to fire the giant AS-3 Kangaroo cruise missile — remain in service with the DA (the strategic arm of the Air Force). Bear C is a maritime reconnaissance version, and Bear E is for strategic reconnaissance. The two principal variants in service with the Soviet naval air arm, the AV-MF, are the Bear D and the more recent Bear F. The Bear D is a specialised maritime reconnaissance aircraft, which in addition to general surveillance duties can provide mid-course guidance to long-range anti-ship missiles such as the SS-N-3 and SS-N-12. The Bear D is therefore a key element in the over-the-horizon (OTH) targeting solution adopted by the Soviet Navy for its surface warships and cruise missile submarines (SSG/SSGN). The weapons bay of the Bear D is occupied by a massive radome exceeded in size only by that of the Western AWACS aircraft, and there are some 40 other aerials, blisters or fairings, the exact configuration varying from aircraft to aircraft. Some 45 Bear Ds are estimated to be in service, and these operate regularly from Cuba and Conakry (West Africa) as well as from Soviet bases.

The Bear F (Tu-142) was built in the 1970s in answer to a requirement for a long-range ASW aircraft. It can be distinguished from other variants by its longer forward fuselage, and the lengthened inboard nacelles. The ventral radome is smaller than that of the Bear D, and stores bays are located in the rear fuselage in place of the underside barbette. Some 40 Bear Fs are thought to be operational.

Below: A Tu-20 Bear C maritime reconnaissance aircraft. The Bear C can be distinguished from the later Bear D by the absence of the large belly radome of the latter. The tail turret houses twin 23mm cannon.

Tupolev Tu-22 Blinder

Type: (Blinder B) land-based strike bomber; (Blinder C) reconnaissance bomber (crew of 3 all versions).

Dimensions: Length 136ft 2in (41·5m); span 91ft 10in (28m); height 34ft (10·4m).

Weight: Empty 88,185lb (40,000kg); maximum 185,185lb (84,000kg).

Engines: Two 28,660lb (13,000kg) thrust Koliesev VD-7 turbojets with afterburners.

Performance: Maximum speed 800kt (1,480km/h) at altitude; service ceiling 60,000ft (18,288m); maximum range 2,160nm (4,000km).

Payload: 1 23mm gun in tail; (Blinder B) 1 AS-4 Kitchen ASM under fuselage.

History: First flight 1959; service delivery (Blinder A) 1963.

Users: USSR (AV-MF).

The Tu-22 (bureau designation Tu-105) Blinder was one of the world's first supersonic bombers. The crew of three are seated in tandem, glass windows for the navigator being provided on either side of the fuselage behind the main radar. In the Blinder B variant the radar is a different type with acquisition/guidance functions for the large AS-4 Kitchen tactical cruise missile, which has a range estimated at 248nm (460km). The latter is carried beneath the fuselage, the outer panels of the bomb doors being removed to accommodate it. The Blinder C reconnaissance variant has an additional search radar in the tail, and carries cameras and EW systems in its bomb bay. It is used for ELINT surveillance and has a limited weapons capability

Some 250 Blinders are thought to have been built, and about 100 of

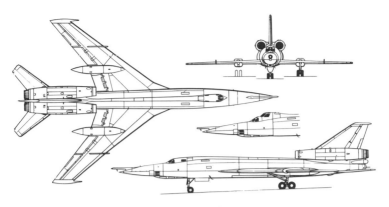

Above: Three-view of a Tu-22 Blinder A (plus nose view of "D").

these were allocated to the AV-MF. There is some disagreement among commentators as to how many of the latter remain in service, and there is also disagreement as to whether the AV-MF operates the "B" variant. Figures for aircraft currently in service vary between 50 Blinder C and up to 80 of both types. They serve exclusively in the areas of the Baltic and Black Sea Fleets. The Blinder is somewhat short on endurance for maritime operations, but served as the basis of the Backfire swing-wing bomber. Early Backfire prototypes, designated Tu-22M, are thought to have been Blinder conversions.

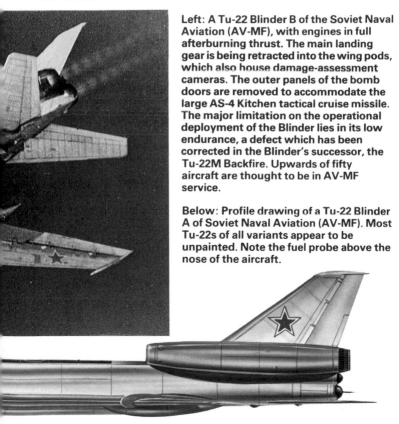

Left: A Tu-22 Blinder B of the Soviet Naval Aviation (AV-MF), with engines in full afterburning thrust. The main landing gear is being retracted into the wing pods, which also house damage-assessment cameras. The outer panels of the bomb doors are removed to accommodate the large AS-4 Kitchen tactical cruise missile. The major limitation on the operational deployment of the Blinder lies in its low endurance, a defect which has been corrected in the Blinder's successor, the Tu-22M Backfire. Upwards of fifty aircraft are thought to be in AV-MF service.

Below: Profile drawing of a Tu-22 Blinder A of Soviet Naval Aviation (AV-MF). Most Tu-22s of all variants appear to be unpainted. Note the fuel probe above the nose of the aircraft.

Tupolev Tu-22M Backfire

Type: (Backfire B) land-based strike bomber (crew of 4).
Dimensions: Length (minus probe) 132ft (40·2m); span (20°) 113ft (34·5m), (55°) 86ft (26·2m); height 33ft (10·1m).
Weight: (Estimated) empty 119,930lb (54,400kg); maximum 268,960lb (122,000kg).
Engines: Probably two Kuznetsov NK-144 turbofans.
Performance: Maximum speed 1,147kt (2,125km/h) at altitude, 594kt (1,100km/h) at sea level: service ceiling 62,355ft (19,000m); range 6,500nm (12,000km); unrefuelled combat radius over 2,000nm (3,700km).
Payload: 2 23mm cannon in remotely-controlled tail barbette; 1 AS-4 or AS-6 ASM under fuselage or 2 AS-4 or AS-6 on wing pylons, or various stores on external fuselage racks.
History: First flight (prototype) 1969;(Tu-22M) 1972; service delivery (Backfire B) 1975.
Users: USSR (AV-MF).

The Backfire was developed from the Tu-22 Blinder. The major shortcoming of the latter, particularly in the maritime strike role, was its limited range and endurance. The adoption of a variable-geometry configuration for its successor was the obvious answer to the requirement for a large, economical cruise radius combined with high performance in the strike role. The production model, the Backfire B, is thought to have been developed via a

Above: This Swedish Air Force photo of a Tu-22M Backfire B of the AV-MF shows a version of the AS-4 Kitchen tactical cruise missile semi-recessed beneath the fuselage. The newer AS-6 Kingfish missile can also be carried beneath the fuselage or on the underwing pylons. Two cannon are carried in the tail for self-defence.

modified Blinder, and a Backfire A model which entered service in limited numbers in 1974. Unlike the Blinder, which has large turbojets on either side of the tail, the Backfire has its engines integrated into the after part of the fuselage, with long inlet ducts forward of the wings. The four-man crew is also seated in different fashion, with the pilot and co-pilot side by side, and the navigator and a systems operator behind them. A single AS-4 Kitchen or AS-6 Kingfish missile can be carried in a recess beneath the fuselage, and there is a remotely-controlled barbette for two 23mm cannon in the tail.

The Backfire is a formidable aircraft by any standards. Its unrefuelled combat radius enables it to strike at shipping in and beyond the GIUK (Greenland-Iceland-UK) gap, and with mid-flight refuelling it could threaten NATO convoys in the North Atlantic. A production rate of 30 aircraft per year was anticipated in the mid-1970s, and some 250 Backfire Bs are thought to have entered service with the AV-MF up to 1983. Somewhat surprisingly, early AV-MF models appear to have been allocated to the Pacific Fleet area, and not to the Northern Fleet area as might have been expected.

Below: The emergence of the Tu-22M Backfire maritime bomber in the late 1970s extended the threat to NATO shipping from the Norwegian Sea into the North Atlantic. The adoption of variable geometry gives the Backfire an impressive cruising radius combined with the ability to make strikes at supersonic speeds — a feature made necessary by the formidable air defence capabilities of the Western carrier battle groups. In this view the wings are in the "half-swept" position. A refuelling probe is apparently a standard fitting.

Below: A Tu-22M Backfire B of the AV-MF. Note the long inlet ducts, and the AS-4 missile semi-recessed beneath the fuselage.

Lockheed F-104 Starfighter

Type: (F-104G) single-seat land-based strike fighter; (RF-104G) reconnaissance aircraft.

Dimensions: Length 54ft 9in (16·69m); span (without tip tanks) 21ft 11in (6·68m); height 13ft 6in (4·1m).

Weight: Empty 14,080lb (6,387kg); maximum 28,779lb (13,054kg).

Engines: One 15,800lb (7,165kg) thrust General Electric J79-11A single-shaft turbojet with afterburner.

Performance: Maximum speed 1,258kt (2,330km/h); service ceiling 58,000ft (17,680m); range 1,200nm (2,222km); combat radius 260nm (482km).

Payload: Centreline rack rated at 2,000lb (907kg) and 2 underwing pylons each rated at 1,000lb (454kg); additional stations (2 underwing and 2 wing-tip) for small AAMs.

History: First flight (XF-104) Feb 1954; (F-104A) Feb 1956; (F-104G) Oct 1960.

Users: FRG (Marineflieger).

The F-104 Starfighter was developed as a result of experience in the Korean War. The emphasis was on high performance, even at the expense of range,

Below: An F-104G Starfighter of the West German Marineflieger fires a Kormoran anti-ship missile. Kormoran, which has a range of 20nm (37km), will also arm the F-104's replacement in the maritime strike role, the Tornado. In the event of hostilities between NATO and the Warsaw Pact, the German maritime strike squadrons would be deployed against Soviet amphibious assault forces and other shipping in the Baltic. Until recently the Marineflieger operated 100 F-104/RF-104s.

weapons and electronic equipment. The result was a high-speed tactical fighter with an exceptionally small wing area. The Starfighter was adopted by a number of other air forces, many of the later variants being specifically tailored to the strike/recce role. Some 1,400 aircraft were built under licence abroad in addition to the models built in the United States. The F-104G, of which 970 were built by a European consortium and a further 110 by Canadair, was a complete redesign to meet the requirements of the German Luftwaffe for a tactical nuclear strike and reconnaissance aircraft. Besides certain structural differences the F-104G introduced the Nasarr multi-mode radar, and inertial navigation.

As the F-4 Phantom entered service in increasing numbers with the Luftwaffe, F-104G Starfighters were transferred to the naval air arm, the Marineflieger, which was tasked with defending the Baltic coastline of the Federal Republic against the threat posed by the amphibious forces and small missile-armed strike craft of the countries of the Warsaw Pact. Two

Below: An F-104G in the colours of the German Marineflieger. Note wing-tip fuel tanks.

squadrons (MFG 1 & 2) comprising some 75 F-104G strike aircraft and 25 RF-104G reconnaissance aircraft were based just south of Denmark (at Schleswig and Eggebek respectively). Since 1977 a number of F-104Gs have converted from the AS 30 anti-ship missile to the new Kormoran, which has a range of 20nm (37km); one Kormoran missile is carried beneath each wing. MFG 1 has now converted to the Tornado IDS and MFG 2 will follow in 1983-84.

USA
Lockheed P-3 Orion

Type: (P-3A, P-3B, P-3C, P-3F, CP-140) long-range maritime patrol aircraft (crew of ten).
Data: P-3C.
Dimensions: Length 116ft 10in (35·61m); span 99ft 8in (30·37m); height 33ft 8½in (10·29m).
Weight: Empty 61,491lb (27,890kg); maximum 142,000lb (64,410kg).
Engines: Four 4,910shp Allison T56-14 single-shaft turboprops.
Performance: Maximum speed 410kt (761km/h); service ceiling 28,300ft (8,625m); range 4,500nm (8,334km); patrol endurance 16 hours.
Payload: Weapons bay for 4 Mk 46 torpedoes, depth bombs, sonobuoys; 4 wing pylons each rated at 2,000lb (907kg) for Mk 46 torpedoes or Harpoon ASMs.
History: First flight (prototype) Aug 1958; (P-3A) April 1961; (P-3C) Sept 1968.
Users: US Navy; Australia, Canada (CP-140), Iran, Japan, Netherlands, New Zealand, Norway, Spain.

In 1957 the US Navy issued a requirement for an "off-the-shelf" LRMP aircraft derived from an established commercial type to replace the P-2 Neptune, which had been in service since World War II. Lockheed's proposal for a conversion of the Electra turboprop airliner was accepted, and the modified aircraft became the P-3A Orion. The commercial airframe was shortened by 12ft (3·65m) and strengthened, equipped for weapons delivery, and given increased fuel capacity. The avionics of the P-3A were simply updated versions of those installed in the Neptune. Some improvements in sensors and displays were made during the P-3A building programme, and further improvements were made in the P-3B, which was also given more powerful engines.

The P-3C, which entered service in 1969, displayed few external differences, but represented a significant advance in ASW capabilities. It incorporated the results of the A-NEW programme (the name derives from "a new concept"), which had been undertaken some ten years previously with a view to revolutionising data handling aboard antisubmarine aircraft. Acoustic operators in earlier aircraft had tended to be overwhelmed by the sheer quantity of sensor data, little of which was usable, and had inadequate time to make effective tactical decisions. This problem was resolved by the introduction of digital computers to record and analyse sensor data. The acoustic operators aboard the P-3C can monitor 16 sonobuoys as compared with half that number in the P-3B, and only four in the P-3A. The nine sonobuoy launch chutes of the P-3A/B have been replaced by 48 externally-loaded chutes, plus a reloadable internal tube. Low-light television (LLTV) replaced the searchlights of earlier aircraft, a FLIR dome replaced the chin gondola for cameras, improvements were made in passive ECM, and installation of the AQS-81 MAD (from the 43rd P-3C) doubled detection range. A general-purpose computer cross-references all these ASW sensors and automatically relates data to position information from an improved navigation system.

The total underwater picture and the aircraft's weapons status are monitored by a Tactical Co-ordinator (TACCO). The communications system incorporates a data link compatible with other P-3C aircraft, and with surface ships and shore bases.

The formidable capabilities of the P-3C are being further increased by a series of update programmes. Update I (in service 1974) included the Omega ▶

Right: One of six P-3Fs delivered to Iran before the fall of the Shah. These were to have carried simplified electronics suitable for maritime patrol, but the final configuration included ASW equipment, including the prominent MAD "stinger" in the tail. It appears that at least one of the six aircraft delivered is still operational. This unusual camouflage scheme was unique to Iranian-operated Orions.

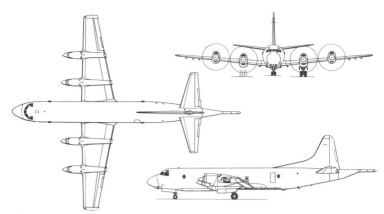

Above: Three-view of a Lockheed P-3C Orion LRMP aircraft.

Above: A P-3 Orion of air test and evaluation squadron VX-1 launches a Harpoon anti-ship missile. Operational P-3Cs are to be fitted with Harpoon to give them a stand-off capability against Soviet surface ships operating in the GIUK gap.

navigation system, a new tactical display for the acoustic operators, and a six-fold increase in computer memory. Update II (1978) incorporates an improved acoustic recording system, provision for firing the Harpoon ASM, FLIR (in place of LLTV), and a sonobuoy reference system similar to that of the S-3 Viking.

Deliveries of the Orion are now over the 500 mark. The US Navy operates 24 active VP squadrons each with nine P-3C Update aircraft, plus 13 Naval Reserve squadrons with older P-3A/Bs. P-3Bs are also operated by New Zealand (5), Norway (7) and Australia (10). Australia's P-3Bs are to be replaced by a similar number of P-3Cs, and a further ten P-3Cs are already in service with the Australian Air Force, while the Netherlands has 13 P-3Cs on order. Iran has six similar P-3Fs, and Japan is building 42 P-3Cs under licence (in

Below: A P-3C Orion Update II of the Australian Air Force. The Australians have purchased ten P-3Cs outright, and are trading in their older P-3Bs for the new model. The P-3C represents a major increase in ASW capabilities.

addition to three aircraft recently delivered by Lockheed) as replacements for her fleet of ageing Kawasaki P-2Js (see pages 136-7). Canada has now replaced her fleet of 26 CP-121 Argus LRMP aircraft with 18 new CP-140 Auroras. The Aurora is a variant of the P-3C built to Canadian specifications, and incorporates the complete sensor and processing systems of the S-3A Viking. The tactical cabin aft of the flight deck has been completely rearranged, with three consoles each for two operators.

Below: A P-3A Orion of VP-4 "Skinny Dragons". More than 200 P-3s are in first-line service with the US Navy.

OTHER SUPER-VALUE MILITARY GUIDES IN THIS SERIES......

OTHER ILLUSTRATED MILITARY GUIDES NOW AVAILABLE . .

Allied Fighters of World War II
Bombers of World War II
German, Italian and Japanese Fighters
of World War II
Modern Fighters and
Attack Aircraft
Modern Soviet Navy

Modern Submarines
Modern Tanks
Modern US Navy
Modern Warships
Pistols and Revolvers
Rifles and Sub-Machine Guns
World War II Tanks

✳ Each has 160 fact-filled pages
✳ Each is colourfully illustrated with hundreds of action photographs
  and technical drawings
✳ Each contains concisely presented data and accurate descriptions
  of major international weapons
✳ Each represents tremendous value

If you would like further information of any of our titles please write to:
Publicity Dept. (Military Div.), Salamander Books Ltd.
52 Bedford Row, London WC1R 4LR